SASL Journal

Volume 1, Number 1
Fall/Winter
2017

A Society for American Sign Language Publication
ISSN: 2474-8277 (online)

SASL Journal
Volume 1, Number 1

Editor-in-Chief

Jody H. Cripps
Department of Audiology, Speech-Language Pathology & Deaf Studies
Towson University
8000 York Rd. Towson, MD 21252
jcripps@towson.edu
Fax: 410 704-4131

Copyeditors

Betsy McDonald
Georgetown University (Retired)

Sheryl B. Cooper
Towson University

Andrew P. J. Byrne
Framingham State University

SASL Board of Directors

Samuel J. Supalla - President
University of Arizona

Deirdre Schlehofer - Vice President
Rochester Institute of Technology

Andrew P. J. Byrne - Secretary
Framingham State University

Harvey Nathanson - Treasurer
Austin Community College

Gabriel Arellano
Georgetown University

Jody H. Cripps
Towson University

Ronald Fenicle
Montgomery College

Russell S. Rosen
CUNY - Staten Island

Print version © 2019 Clemson University
Print ISBN 978-1-949979-42-8

Copyright © 2017 A Society for American Sign Language Publication.
ISSN 2474-8277 (online)

SASL Journal
Volume 1, Number 1

Table of Contents

Editor's Commentary

SASLJ Unveiled: A New Frontier
Jody H. Cripps 4

Featured Manuscripts

American Sign Language: Access, Benefits, and Quality
Russell S. Rosen 7

A Sketch on Reading Methodology for Deaf Children
Samuel J. Supalla 35

American Sign Language Literature: Some Considerations for Legitimacy and Quality Issues
Andrew P. J. Byrne 56

Understanding Signed Music
Jody H. Cripps and Ely Lyonblum 78

Review

Is Silence Music to the Eye? A Review of Signed Music: A Symphonious Odyssey
Lisalee D. Egbert 96

SASLJ Unveiled: A New Frontier

Jody H. Cripps
Editor-in-Chief

As the editor, I am pleased to announce the inaugural issue of the Society for American Sign Language Journal (SASLJ). This journal marks an important milestone by providing a new viewpoint for signers, both deaf and hearing, living in the United States and Canada. American Sign Language (ASL) has been in use for a long time by deaf people, the primary users of this language. 2017 marks the signed language's 200th anniversary as marked by its origin with the first permanent school for the deaf founded in Hartford, Connecticut in 1817. Numerous people have contributed to the study of ASL over the years, and this journal provides a new platform for past and present work related to promoting the concept of linguistic accessibility. ASL is not merely another language for consideration, but it is a signed language that has ramifications for all aspects and functions of society. Deaf people are not only part of their own cultural community, but they also reside in the larger society as well. Including hearing individuals who are signers will help broaden the view as it shifts emphasis on deafness to a more socially enlightened agenda that encompasses differences, diversity, and inclusiveness. SASLJ is an academic peer-reviewed journal that aims to serve researchers, scholars, administrators, developers, assessors, practitioners, and students to impart and share knowledge towards ASL as a human language.

The first part of this editorial commentary will include a brief historical account of the steps toward creating the Society for American Sign Language (SASL) and its first symposium in 2015. The second half will cover the establishment of SASLJ.

History of SASL as an Organization

The initiation of the SASL organization occurred at *Deaf Studies Today! Conference* in Orem, Utah on the evening of April 2014 at a hotel with approximately 20 to 25 people (scholars and conference participants). There was a discussion on the need for creating an organization that focuses on ASL and its role in current society. A small number of attendees (Drs. Samuel Supalla - Arizona and Jody Cripps - Maryland, Mr. Ronald Fenicle – Maryland, and Harvey Nathanson - Texas) volunteered as the working group to implement the establishment of the organization. This included planning the symposium for the Fall of 2015, and inviting all interested supporters across the country to consider becoming Executive Council (EC) members for this new organization. From this response, nine founding board members emerged (see names in the next paragraph). On September 11, 2015, SASL was formally recognized in the state of Maryland.

SASL's first symposium was given the theme and title: *Celebration of Sign Language: Revisiting Language, Literacy, and Performing Arts.* It was held at Towson University in Towson, Maryland on November 14, 2015. The symposium began with the first EC meeting in the morning with the following members:

- Mr. Gabriel Arellano (Georgetown University)
- Dr. Patrick Boudreault (Gallaudet University)
- Dr. Andrew Byrne (Framingham State University)

- Dr. Jody Cripps (Towson University)
- Mr. Ronald Fenicle (Towson University)
- Dr. Russell Rosen (CUNY - Staten Island)
- Mr. Harvey Nathanson (Austin Community College)
- Dr. Deirdre Schlehofer (Rochester Institute of Technology)
- Dr. Samuel Supalla (University of Arizona)

At this meeting, Dr. Supalla was voted President, myself as Vice President, Dr. Byrne as Secretary, and Mr. Nathanson as Treasurer.

Later in the afternoon, six scholars from the EC presented, beginning with Dr. Boudreault who discussed language preservation regarding Langue des signes québécoise (LSQ, also known as Quebec Sign Language, a signed language used in Quebec, Canada). He talked about LSQ and other signed languages which are declining in use among deaf people (see Dr. Boudreault's article covering a similar topic in SASL's newsletter (Fall 2016 - issue 3)). The second presenter was Dr. Rosen who presented on the rapid growth of ASL classes in high schools, college and universities across the country (which is now published in this first issue of SASLJ). Dr. Supalla talked about a new perspective on reading development issues with deaf children who sign, and he is also published in this SASLJ.

The last three presenters focused on revisiting the performing arts. Dr. Byrne spoke on the importance of original literary works in ASL (also published in this issue). On the topic of ASL poetry analysis, Dr. Schlehofer investigated the interpretation of Clayton Valli's poem *Snowflake* and found that there have been misinterpretations from well-meaning scholars. As the final presenter of the evening, I talked about how music performances made by deaf signers are real and worthy of attention (published in this issue).

After the presentations, Dr. Boudreault led a town hall meeting with the panel and symposium participants. Participants had the opportunity to ask questions regarding the new SASL organization. At this time, the names of SASL's elected officers, EC members, and the date that SASL was recognized as an organization were announced. The EC is now called the Board of Directors. The SASL mission statement was also revealed at the town hall as follows:

> The Society for American Sign Language (SASL) is a professional association with the credentials dedicated to basic and applied research about American Sign Language. SASL's goal is to validate and expand linguistic accessibility. Linguistic principles are emphasized for understanding the signed language along with its aesthetics and role in literacy development and learning. SASL's scope and forum includes theory, policy, and practice considerations, as well as addressing how an alternative language modality fulfills the needs and well-being of all citizens in society.

Creating a Journal

A few months after the symposium, I resigned my position as Vice President of SASL and accepted the role of Editor-in-Chief for SASLJ. Dr. Schlehofer is now the Vice President for SASL. In order to create this journal, I reached out to six symposium presenters, inviting them to write manuscripts for the first issue. Four presenters (including myself) were able to complete and submit manuscripts for review and publication. One of the symposium participants was asked to write a review of the evening performance for this journal issue on the evening performance called *Signed Music: A Symphonious Odyssey* (it can be viewed at https://www.youtube.com/watch?v=2JjFCM8UZHM). This evening performance, which I directed, combined a variety of signed music pieces including video and live performances done by deaf musicians from the United States and Canada.

Each submitted manuscript was reviewed by two reviewers and we received excellent feedback from them. I am pleased that all four submissions were accepted for publication. We also have two copyeditors and an APA expert working with me during the final review process. I sincerely appreciate everyone's hard work for making this first issue a reality. Also, I would like to acknowledge SASL's President Supalla for his support in promoting the implementation of this journal and the Society for ASL Board of Directors for their affirmation and belief in our vision of providing a new journal format for all to enjoy. Finally, I must give my deepest gratitude to the authors who contributed their pieces to this first issue.

And last, I would like to sincerely thank Dr. Lisalee Egbert for completing the invited performance review, which is included at the end of this issue. It is my hope, along with other SASL members, that the articles in this issue will help show critical new perspectives and create more insightful dialogue and beneficial research and scholarship in the future.

American Sign Language: Access, Benefits, and Quality

Russell S. Rosen
CUNY – Staten Island

Abstract

While American Sign Language (ASL) is taught as a bona fide language in general education and used as the language of instruction in schools and programs for the deaf, several issues remain regarding the access to, benefits of, and quality of ASL as a language. This article provides an overview of sign language education, reviews studies on the benefits of using ASL as a language for deaf and hearing learners, and discusses current pedagogical and intervention issues. This is followed by discussion on ideas and options to increase access, benefits and quality assurance for ASL in American society.

Introduction

American Sign Language (ASL) has reached the 200-year mark. The timing could not be better for reflecting on the history and recent years of sign language use in the United States. Despite interest and enrollment in classes where ASL is taught as a language in general education and used as the language of instruction in schools and programs for the deaf, there are challenges and issues that need to be addressed. ASL has been used within the society of predominantly speaking and hearing people. While a majority of speaking and hearing people could have become signers in addition to being speakers, for now they have not. Despite its documented history and use in the deaf community, ASL has been marginalized in the larger American society. This can be seen in the fact that curriculum, instruction, and assessment remain English-based at schools and programs for deaf and hearing children. This effect suggests that the power of spoken language remains unchecked (cf. J. H. Cripps & S. Supalla, 2012).

While ASL may be taught as part of deaf students' learning of scholastic subjects and to meet hearing students' foreign language requirement in high schools, colleges, and universities, it has only been one option for the students. Hearing students may choose languages such as Spanish or French over ASL, for instance, and their potential for becoming signers and being able to communicate with deaf people may not be met. Similarly, schools for the deaf may hold out using ASL with deaf students as only one option, and students' potential for learning scholastic subjects may also not be met. Such a language situation for deaf and hearing children in schools constitutes the focus for this paper.

This paper seeks to generate a more comprehensive picture on the status of ASL for two groups of learners (one being deaf and the other hearing). The scope of ASL within the deaf community dominates the scholarly literature with very little attention to hearing people who sign. Giving these two groups of people a more equitable treatment provides insights and considerations that may be highly valuable. It is also important to keep in mind that deaf children who sign would be learning English as a second language, which has repercussions for their scholastic learning. For instance, reading and writing difficulties with English for deaf children have been reported and must be addressed (Chamberlain & Mayberry, 2000; Hoffmeister & Caldwell-Harris, 2014).

The questions for this paper are: 1) How accessible is ASL for deaf and hearing learners?, 2) What merits are there in learning and using ASL?, and 3) How effective is the delivery and usage of ASL in the education system? Challenges and issues concerning ASL and society will be addressed with new ideas on how to maximize access, benefits, and quality of ASL with individuals, families, and the education system.

Access to American Sign Language in Education

To frame the ensuing discussion on access to ASL for deaf individuals and for individuals who are hearing, a history of ASL in the U.S. with the deaf and hearing populations and in educational institutions is provided.

History of ASL in the Education of Deaf Students

ASL was initially developed for use among individuals who are deaf at the schools for the deaf in the early nineteenth century. Prior to the establishment of the first schools for the deaf, there were indigenous sign language systems that were already in use in certain areas of the U.S. where there was a high prevalence of deafness among inhabitants. Martha's Vineyard, an island off the Massachusetts coast is a prime example, since it played a role in the development of ASL (Bahan & Poole-Nash, 1996; Groce, 1985). The fact that both deaf and hearing residents on Martha's Vineyard were signers is a rarity. Although hearing island residents spoke English, they often signed with each other and with deaf residents. Successful inclusion and respect for diversity concerning deaf people was practiced on the island until the demise of this signing society in the twentieth century (Groce, 1985).

On the U.S. mainland, the attitude about sign language was that hearing people were strictly speakers, an attitude that continues to characterize the country to this day. This has resulted in the restricted use of ASL in schools for the deaf. The first such school, the Connecticut Asylum for the Instruction of Deaf-Mutes (now the American School for the Deaf), was established in Hartford, Connecticut by Laurent Clerc, who hailed from France, and helped establish the school along with Thomas Hopkins Gallaudet, an Episcopalian priest who became interested in educating deaf children after his encounter with a deaf girl in his neighborhood. At the school, Clerc imported French Sign Language, which became Anglicized, that is, French signs for English words, and curricula from his previous position at the Royal National Institute for the Education of Deaf-Mutes in Paris, France. The deaf children who constituted the first classes at the Connecticut school brought some signing forms from their individual regions, such as Martha's Vineyard (Lane, Pillard, & French, 2000). At the school, the Anglicized French Sign Language and the indigenous sign languages were merged together and became Old ASL. As time passed, Old ASL underwent changes as expected for any human language, now seen as Modern ASL (T. Supalla & Clark, 2014). This process included the nationwide dissemination of ASL. From the 1810s to the 1850s, 20 schools for the deaf were established, and all of these schools employed the same language, ASL, and used the same curricula. Individuals who wanted to become teachers of the deaf were trained at the Connecticut school and brought ASL to other schools for the deaf (Van Cleve & Crouch, 1989).

This network of schools for the deaf helped with the dissemination and standardization of ASL through its history. The mechanisms for the transmission of ASL to generations of users represent a trait that is unique to the deaf population as well. Normally, a hearing child would learn and master a native language that his or her parents speak. Deaf children with hearing parents are not likely to find ASL readily used in their homes. For most of history (and to some extent still true today), deaf children have relied on schools for the deaf to access ASL. The fact that schools for the deaf were residential was helpful. Erting and Kuntze (2008) explained that the school dormitories served as the sites where deaf children socialized and acquired ASL. Signing staff at the schools played the role of surrogate parents and promoted the transmission of ASL over generations. Although few in number, deaf children from deaf parents who used ASL at home also helped ensure that all deaf children at the school became signers. More discussion on deaf children of deaf parents will follow in the latter part of this paper.

It was not until the latter part of the nineteenth century, when oralism took hold in most deaf schools, that the language of instruction was changed from ASL to spoken, i.e., oral and aural, English. As history confirms, signing and sign language itself could not be eradicated, due to deaf individuals' natural desire to become signers. The human capacity for language underlies the power of ASL for deaf individuals. The introduction of oralism began with the establishment of day schools for the deaf in metropolitan areas in the mid-nineteenth century. The proliferation of oralism within schools for the deaf occurred after it was given legitimization as a language of pedagogy at the International Conference in the Education of the Deaf in Milan, Italy in 1880 (Baynton, 1996). There were a variety of responses to oralism in schools for the deaf in America (Van Cleve & Couch, 1989). One response was that the schools, such as the Nebraska School for the Deaf, transformed from completely manual to completely oral. The second response was the establishment of two separate departments within a school, such as the Pennsylvania School for the Deaf, a manualist department, and an oralist department. The third response was that schools, such as the New York School for the Deaf, maintained its manualist approach, but offered a number of classes in articulation.

During the rise and dominance of oralism in the field of deaf education, ASL went underground. However, it was the continuing operation of schools for the deaf where deaf students assembled and learned ASL regardless of the policy. Oralism was strongest when in the classroom. The dorm settings and playgrounds at the deaf schools continued to provide opportunities for deaf students for a signing environment. Clearly, the cost of diverting deaf education from signing to speaking was enormous and counter-intuitive. Had history been different and more accommodating to sign language, perhaps developments like a writing system for ASL could have been facilitated. Nover and Ruiz (1995) are correct in pointing out the importance of language planning for ASL, especially in its codification. Only recently (in the 21st century) have educators and scholars debated the question of ASL literacy and directions for how ASL should be represented on paper (Grushkin, 2017; Hopkins, 2008; Miller, 2001; Rosen, Hartman, & Wang, 2017; S. Supalla, J. H. Cripps, & Byrne, 2017; van der Hulst & Channon, 2010).

Beyond the pre-college level, Gallaudet University also played an important role for ASL as a language when established as the National Deaf-Mute College in 1865. Deaf students from all corners of the U.S. came to study, exchanging and homogenizing local signs, and bringing new signs home to their local deaf communities. Through Gallaudet graduates, ASL became a national sign language, although some regional dialects persisted. It was not until the 1960s that ASL linguistic structures began to be researched by linguists (Stokoe, 1960; Stokoe, Casterline, & Croneberg, 1965), and ASL was proven to be a bona fide language by the 1980s (Klima & Bellugi, 1979; Liddell, 1980; Padden, 1981; Wilbur, 1979). ASL, in spite of its distinct modality from spoken languages, shares linguistic features that are universal for spoken languages (Fischer & Siple, 1990; Fromkin, 1988; Neidle, Kegel, MacLaughlin, Bahan, & Lee, 2000; Sandler & Lillo-Martin, 2006). William C. Stokoe, a professor at Gallaudet University, was credited with starting sign language research work. This validation of ASL, coupled with the civil rights movement by deaf people that commenced with the Deaf President Now movement at Gallaudet University in 1988 (Christensen & Barnartt, 2003), resulted in sign language returning as the language of instruction in many schools and programs for deaf children.

At present, the idea of deaf children and adults being signers may be widely accepted, but it does not mean that society's support for ASL is strong or absolute. There continue to be forces that undermine ASL as a language. This is especially true concerning the current handling of the cochlear implant technology. Humphries, Kushalnagar, Mathur, Napoliu, Padden, Rathmann, and Smith (2012) examined the medical professionals and practices and argue that they have not proactively supported ASL for families with deaf children. Humphries et al. were alarmed by the increase in cochlear implantation of deaf children and the emphasis on speech and hearing training. They noted the limited critical period of brain plasticity for exposure to a natural language. If delayed, subsequent development of cognitive activities that rely on solid natural language acquisition may be limited. They also noted that the cochlear implant surgery has provided limited success within the deaf child population.

Consequently, this emphasis on speech-exclusive approaches and the uneven success with cochlear implantation have created harmful effects on deaf children. The harmful effects for deaf children include linguistic deprivation and communication maltreatment. Humphries et al. argue that the medical professionals need to be truthful to and build trust with parents and deaf children. To prevent harmful effects, Humphries et al. suggest that the medical professionals and parents consider alternatives to speech-exclusive approaches. They propose remedies such as the use of sign language including ASL, and adjusting expectations of cochlear implant results.

History of Teaching ASL to Hearing Students

While the teaching of ASL to hearing students has a much shorter history as compared to deaf education, one must appreciate the fact that Thomas Hopkins Gallaudet was a student of sign language. He learned the language informally through interactions with deaf individuals. The modern idea of a hearing person wanting to study ASL and easily taking a course at a college or university, for instance, had not developed. Moreover, the positive attitude that Gallaudet had about sign language must be described as an exception to the rule. In fact, oralism dominated deaf education during the late nineteenth century and for most of the twentieth century. This suggests that society had strong and negative opinions about signing or sign language.

While it may appear that society has changed towards supporting ASL, this situation also appears to be somewhat contradictory. This is evidenced by deaf children receiving cochlear implants, who frequently do not have an opportunity to learn and use ASL. This state of affairs is testimony to the persistence of the social problem. One must also look critically at the description of ASL as a foreign language for study with hearing students. While ASL is most definitely an American language, it is put in a category with Spanish, French, and other foreign languages taught in the educational system. The sign language situation in the United States is complicated, and support for ASL is difficult to pinpoint.

At the same time, the foreign language status for ASL allows more people in society to learn it than ever before. This stands as a valuable attribute. Social science research that has documented the American deaf community and culture (Davis, 1998; Frishberg, 1988; Padden & Humphries, 1988, 2005; Rutherford, 1988; Wilcox, 1992) is what empowered scholars and advocates to seek the adoption of ASL as a part of "foreign" or "world" language curricula. The number of states that formally recognize ASL as a foreign language has grown, beginning with 28 states in 1997 (Kreeft-Peyton, 1998) 32 in 1999 (Jacobowitz, 1999), 38 in 2004 (Gallaudet Research Institute, 2004) and 45 in 2014 (Rosen, 2015). The results of deaf community work in ensuring recognition of ASL and deaf community and culture at the state government level were carried over to high schools, colleges and universities (Rosen, 2006).

Colleges and universities. ASL as second (L2) or additional (L*n*) language was initially offered in colleges and universities in conjunction with collegiate programs that prepare individuals to work with deaf children or adults. In particular, these classes were developed in the fields of deaf education, speech pathology and vocational rehabilitation. The broader idea of studying ASL as part of meeting the foreign language requirement took over and shaped the educational landscape in a profound way. It did not matter if students had plans to work with deaf children or adults. ASL was now seen as a language worthy of study in itself.

The rise of ASL for study by hearing students has been documented in various scholarly sources. Shroyer and Holmes (1982) identified five higher education institutions in 1980 that accepted ASL in fulfillment of requirements for proficiency in a foreign language. McIntire (1984) listed eight higher education institutions in 1983 that did not teach sign language but accepted it in fulfillment of foreign language requirements, which increased to 12 in the following year (*The Reflector*, 1984). Delgado (1984) added that there were 20 higher education institutions that accepted sign language in fulfillment of the foreign language requirement for their graduates.

A study by Corwin and Wilcox (1985) attempted to ascertain policies on ASL as a foreign language from over one hundred higher education institutions. Most of the universities reported that they did recognize ASL as a language but did not accept it as suitable for foreign language credit. Since then, this resistance seems to have lessened. Wilcox and Wilcox (1991) found that ASL was accepted as one of the foreign languages that meet the requirement for undergraduate admission in 48 U.S. national research universities as of 1991. The number had grown to 93 in 1997 (Cooper, 1997), 148 in 2006 (Wilcox, 2006), and to 181 by 2015 (Wilcox, 2015). Delgado (1984) took a national survey of community and junior colleges, and found that 373 institutions offered sign language classes.

Goldberg, Looney, and Lusin (2015) produced some of the most solid findings. This group of researchers conducted a survey of foreign language enrollments in higher education for the Modern Language Association and found that 756 (a third) of colleges and universities in 2013 offered ASL classes. In addition, an increasing number of colleges and universities offer formal degree programs in ASL Studies with coursework not only in ASL but also ASL linguistics, history, sociology and the anthropology of deaf community and culture, and ASL and Deaf arts and literature. Goldberg and his colleagues added that the number of higher education institutions that offer bachelor's degrees for ASL majors has increased from 28 undergraduate colleges and universities in 2005-2006, to 35 in 2008-2009, and 43 in 2012-2013.

High schools. The impetus for introducing ASL for foreign language credit in public high schools was the presence of signing deaf students in mainstream classrooms. According to Rosen (2006), the mainstreaming of ASL and deaf community and culture was initially framed by Individuals with Disabilities Education Act (IDEA) provisions and practices that promoted the use of speech and hearing for students with deafness. This legislation covers what is known as special education, which is a powerful force in the public school system. A pathological orientation towards deafness was criticized in the scholarly literature as "audist," and places spoken language in a superior position (Bauman, 2004; Eckert & Rowley, 2013; Lane, 1992). This attitude has created communication and language barriers between deaf and hearing students in public education classrooms (Foster, 1989; Gaustad & Kluwin, 1992; Stinson & Liu, 1999). In the 1997 and 1999 reauthorizations of IDEA, revisions were made by deleting references to speech and hearing difficulties and their role in receiving linguistic information, and by including "language preferences" of deaf students, including sign language. ASL was mentioned as one of the languages used by deaf students for the first time in the 1999 reauthorization of IDEA (Rosen, 2006).

Consequently, one of the altered IDEA practices with signing deaf students was the increased presence of sign language interpreters with signing deaf students in mainstreamed settings. Their presence generated interest among hearing students and teachers in the lives, experiences, language, community, and culture of the signing deaf students. Hearing students began to increasingly request courses in ASL (Rosen, 2006). As a result, general education schools began to accept ASL as one of their languages. In terms of the number and percentage of high schools in the U.S. that offer ASL for foreign language credit, a national survey conducted by the Center for Applied Linguistics (CAL) showed that in 1996 ASL was offered in 1% of the 1,650 surveyed US secondary schools with foreign language programs, or 17 high schools, in 1987, and 2%, or 33 high schools, in 1997 (CAL, 1997). Rosen (2008) found that out of about 1,900 public high schools in the U.S. that offered foreign language classes in 2004, 701 offered ASL for foreign language credit.

Benefits of ASL for Learning

In this section, the attention shifts to understanding what benefits there are in learning ASL. The value of sign language competency is addressed first with deaf students and then hearing students.

Deaf Students

The value of ASL for deaf students is examined in relation to their cognitive and language development. This includes consideration of how deaf students' sign language competency helps with their learning of other languages.

Language development. In order for deaf children to be able to develop language and cognitive skills, they need to first acquire linguistic principles. The relevance of ASL as a sign language in this process has emerged as an important consideration since it is something to be seen, not heard (Singleton, S. Supalla, Litchfield, & Schley, 1998). The early perceptions that deaf children have language problems gave way to the emerging idea that the problem lies with English as a spoken language. Supporting this, ASL acquisition studies (Mayberry & Eichen, 1991; Meier, 1991; Meier & Newport, 1990; Newport & Meier, 1985) demonstrated that acquiring sign language provides deaf children with knowledge about the nature of language. Newport and Meier (1985) reviewed studies on ASL acquisition by deaf children and found that the stages of acquisition are similar to hearing children's acquisition of spoken English in American society. Both deaf children's acquisition of ASL and hearing children's acquisition of spoken English undergo similar stages, which are the following: basic, one-sign, to two-sign and telegraphic grammars, progressing to uninflected forms, and then to inflected forms and adult word order forms.

Studies on the acquisition of ASL by deaf children continue to produce positive findings since Newport and Meier's 1985 study. For instance, Lillo-Martin and Pichler (2006) studied the acquisition of verbs; Lillo-Martin (2000) studied the acquisition of wh-questions; Pettito (1994) studied the acquisition of pronouns; and Reilly, McIntire, and Bellugi (1990) studied the acquisition of grammaticalized facial expressions in ASL. These studies demonstrated that the acquisition of ASL is a step-wise process that is similar to the acquisition of English, although modality differences between ASL and English are found in some aspects, particularly involving the use of space to mark references and locations.

The critical period for language development is an important consideration regarding deaf children learning ASL, as well as for any language, giving children a strong foundation for language and cognitive development. Newport (1990) reported a study she conducted with Ted Supalla in which they tested early and late learners of ASL in the production and comprehension of ASL syntax and morphology in comparison to early learners. They found that early learners produced higher scores than late learners. In addition, late learners produced more errors than early learners in word order and ASL verb forms, producing more frozen than productive sign forms and incorrect word order (Newport, 1990). Boudreault and Mayberry (2006) studied grammatical judgment accuracy of ASL sentence structures for verbs, questions, relative clauses and classifier sentences by groups of deaf subjects of different ages. They found that early learners of ASL performed better and responded more quickly to stimuli than later learners. This suggests that the earlier a child learns ASL, the more fluent the child would be in using the language to converse and comprehend signed conversations. The critical age of acquisition plays a role here: the earlier a child learns ASL, the more skilled the child will be in creating and using language constructions; conversely, the later a child acquires the language, the less skilled the child will be in creating and using the language.

Cognitive development. Other than supporting deaf students in their language development, acquiring ASL also benefits their cognitive development. When deaf children acquire ASL, they also acquire world knowledge and increased awareness of the events and life-scripts in the world around them (cf. Wilbur, 2000). A study by Schick, De Villiers, De Villiers, and Hoffmeister (2007) showed that deaf children who learn ASL at home have superior theory of mind ability, an ability that taps into their conceptions of facts and truths, because ASL helped them to develop robust vocabulary and syntactic complements.

ASL acquisition also aids deaf children's cognitive development in that they have the language needed to perform cognitive operations such as symbolization, categorizations, equivalence, conservation, comparison and referentiality. Neuroscience research on the visual ability and processing of deaf and hearing subjects has shown that ASL has contributed to deaf subjects' increased visual peripheral skills, cognitive operations of spatialization, including spatial mapping and referencing, all cognitive operations that are crucial to language development (Bavelier, Tomann, Hutton, Mitchell, Corina, Liu, & Neville, 2000; Emmorey, 2002). ASL was found to have aided deaf children in their development of spatial concepts and spatial geography. Wilson, Bettiger, Nicula, and Klima (1997) studied how the visual-manual modality of ASL affects the working memory for spatial and temporal information in ASL signers. They compared deaf children who are native users of ASL and hearing children who are native English speakers in their performance of linguistic and alinguistic spatial memory tasks and found that deaf children outperformed hearing children. This suggests that ASL exerts a positive influence on the architecture of spatial working memory within and outside the linguistic domain.

The visual requirements for ASL processing have effects on the processing of peripheral visual stimuli. In attention tasks with deaf native users of ASL, electroencephalogram (or EEG) tracing of their brain showed enhanced brain waves in the part of the brain that is known to process sound processing, suggesting that the vision area of the brain in the deaf native ASL users has spread and is allocated to the acoustic areas to enhance attention to visual stimuli, even if hearing is absent, and this has enabled peripheral processing over wider space (Pettito, Zatorre, Gauna, Nikelski, Dostie, & Evans, 2000). Thus, deaf native ASL users were able to detect peripheral movements to a greater extent than hearing native spoken English users. The study showed that deaf native ASL users performed better than the hearing native spoken English users in processing and integrating visual information (Codina, Buckley, Port, & Pascalis, 2011). Visual processing via ASL also has effects on deaf native users' ability to identify faces. In studies of face recognition with different orientations and shading, deaf native users performed better than hearing native users of spoken English (Bettiger et al., 1997).

Other studies showed that deaf native child users of ASL performed better in tasks such as image generation and rotation, block assembly, digit span and spatial span; recognizing faces, detecting peripheral movement, and integrating rapidly presented visual information (Edwards, Figueras, Mellanby, & Langdon, 2011; Emmorey, Corina, & Bellugi, 1995; Emmorey, Kosslyn, & Bellugi, 1993; Hauser, Cohen, Dye, & Bavelier, 2007; Wilson et al., 1997). ASL users were shown to be adept at generating and transforming mental images in nonlinguistic mental image generation task experiments with superimposition and flash-pacing of the letter 'x' on a grid (Emmorey et al., 1995). They were also adept in mental image rotation, such as the task of using stimuli and deciding whether the response is its mirror image or the same shape when the image is rotated (Emmorey et al., 1993). They were also more adept than hearing peers in the Block Design Subtest in WISC-R in which they created 3-D blocks of cubes to match as stimulus blocks of cubes (Sisco & Anderson, 1980).

Learning other languages. When the acquisition of ASL occurs earlier in deaf children's lives, it will not only facilitate their cognitive and language development, but also provides a solid foundation for their learning of other languages as second or additional languages. A group of scholars at Gallaudet University wrote a seminal paper called "Unlocking the Curriculum: Achieving Access for Deaf Students" (Johnson, Liddell, & Erting, 1989), a work that opened up a nationwide dialogue on the topic of ASL and deaf children's education. English literacy was included in the paper. The description of English as a written language for deaf children after ASL acquisition was a radical concept at the time. The status of English as a second language or L2 requires a new way of thinking for the field of deaf education.

As scholars in the field of second and additional language acquisition know, learning other languages is not a simple matter of translating from one language to another by matching one-word for one-word, or one phrasal structure for one phrasal structure, across languages. This is because languages do not share similar vocabularies, phrasal structures and word orders (Hawkins, 2001). Likewise, deaf children will have to know the differences between English and the language that they know, ASL. They cannot read English fluently when they have no idea about the language differences.

L2 acquisition studies also indicate that linguistic features shared by all languages comprise the Universal Grammar of all languages (Hawkins, 2001). Under the Universal Grammar model, all languages consist of phonology, lexicon, phrases and word orders. Universal Grammar also holds that languages differ in the details of these phonological systems, lexical items, phrasal structures, and word orders. Cross-language similarities and differences have repercussions for second and additional language learning. Comparative analysis lessons would serve as a good way of teaching deaf students about English to allow them read the text and familiarize themselves with English.

The consideration of how all languages share phonological constructs, while differing in phonemes, is important. Deaf students will need to first learn about ASL phonemes. In contrast to English phonemes, signs consist of parts in the form of handshape, location, movement and palm orientation. With this in mind, it is natural for hearing students to enjoy accessing English phonology due to their capacity of hearing the language. While not accessing the English language in the same way, deaf students will nevertheless understand that English phonology operates according to the same general principles of word structure found with ASL phonology. Deaf students will need to work around their inability to hear and process spoken words. They can see English words in print and will need to focus on developing spelling skills. Fingerspelling may come in handy as a tool to develop spelling skills.

For other aspects of deaf students learning English, all languages share similar lexical categories, which are nouns, verbs, adjectives and prepositions, and similar phrases, which are verb phrases, noun phrases, adjective phrases and preposition phrases. They differ in functional categories consisting of lexical items that tie phrases together into sentences, and they include copulas, auxiliaries, plurality, and inflections (affixes). Deaf students knowing how ASL works as a language will be prepared for learning what is specific to English. This includes being aware that each sign in ASL and word in English have multiple meanings. These students will then choose words to fit meanings rather than signs and, vice versa, perform signs to fit meanings rather than words.

Within phrases, all languages have specifiers to mark subjects, heads to mark lexical items, and complements to mark lexical categories. Languages differ in the ordering of specifier, head and complement in their phrasal structures. Regarding language differences in the ordering of specifier, head and complement in phrasal structures, English follows the specifier-head-complement order; French follows the specifier-complement-head order; and ASL follows both specifier-head-complement and complement-specifier-head orders. For instance, in English we say "John has a red car;" in French we say "John has a car red;" and in ASL we sign either JOHN HAS RED CAR, or RED CAR JOHN HAS. Deaf students will need to attend to the ordering of specifiers, heads and complements of phrasal structures. This is a cognitive process, not a simple sign-for-word and word-for-sign learning.

Languages also differ in the order of words and phrases in sentences. Cross-linguistic cognitive studies show that all languages have different cognitive organization of information pertaining to the relationship between entities (nouns), attributes (adjectives), locations (prepositions) and movements (verbs) that generate different phrasal structures and word orders (Jarvis & Pavlenko, 2008; Langacker, 1987). For instance, picture a ball on a table, and compare ASL and English preposition phrases. English and ASL differ in the relationship between movement and location. In English movement precedes location and in ASL location precedes movement. In English we say "the ball is on the table," where the noun phrase precedes the preposition phrase, tied together by a copula "is." In ASL, we sign TABLE BALL BALL-ON-TABLE, where the preposition phrase precedes the noun phrase, and does not require the "is" copula. Deaf students would not be able to master English word and phrasal orders if they learn it by matching it with the word and phrasal orders of ASL. They must understand how languages differ in the way they conceptualize and organize notions of entities, nouns, attributes, locations and movements, and how they order grammatical components.

What has been discussed thus far has support through research. Regarding deaf children's learning of English, research studies of deaf students show that a few of them rely on sound-based phonological awareness to process print instructional materials. A meta-analytic study conducted by Mayberry, del Giudice, and Lieberman (2011) found 57 studies that experimentally tested phonological coding and awareness (PCA) skills in thousands of deaf participants. Half of the studies found statistically significant evidence for PCA skills in deaf students. However, only 11% of the variance in reading proficiency of deaf participants was predicted by PCA skills. Instead, language ability affected 35% of the variance in reading proficiency. Thus, based on the study, reading achievement in deaf individuals was not based on PCA skills. Language ability had a greater influence on reading ability.

Additionally, Williams (1999) found that deaf children use sign language as they read and write in order to engage in representational, directive, interactional, personal, and heuristic use of language to support their writing endeavors with English. This is not surprising as ASL is deaf children's native and accessible language. Wilbur (2000) implored that learning ASL will not affect or interfere with the development of English literacy skills; instead, it can contribute to higher literacy and cognitive skills. It is at the cognitive-semantic level, rather than the linguistic level, that deaf child users of ASL bridge into English as their second language.

Other studies point to significant positive correlations between ASL usage and English language skills. Prinz and Strong (1998; 2000), and Ausbrooks (2007) studied language interdependence between ASL and English within the context of reading comprehension skills. They found a statistically significant relationship between ASL morphology and semantics and English reading comprehension, reading vocabulary, and overall English language skills. Hoffmeister (2000) found that students with intensive ASL exposure scored significantly higher on all ASL measures, the SAT Reading Comprehension subtest, and on the Rhode Island Test of Language Structure than those with more limited exposure. Kuntze (2004) investigated the ASL and English skills of deaf students, and found that the skill levels of ASL in their rendition of reading passages in printed English significantly predicted their comprehension of the passages. Smith (2007) found that students with higher English reading comprehension scores also scored statistically significantly better on ASL phonology, morphology, syntax, semantic, and pragmatic tasks on the Test of American Sign Language Abilities—Receptive. These studies show that the language ability of the students in using and comprehending ASL has the potential to carry over as language ability in comprehending English-printed reading.

Padden and Ramsey (1998), De Garcia (2003), and Padden (2006) pointed out that merely knowing a sign language does not support the development of English literacy, but that tying specific elements of it to English print supports reading and writing in deaf signing individuals. Hoffmeister, Philip, Costello, and Grass (1997) found that students' manipulation of certain linguistic elements of ASL (e.g. classifiers, plurals, and verbs of motion and location) were directly transferred to understanding of specific syntactical elements of English. The researchers argued that continued development of both languages generated cognitive and linguistic benefits, and that linguistic proficiencies in one language can be transferred to another language. For this to occur, proficiency in one language, say ASL, is needed to facilitate second language learning, such as in English. For the researchers, it was important that deaf children possess metalinguistic knowledge of the languages so that they can transfer literacy skills across the languages.

When ASL is used in classrooms with deaf students, it serves as an intervention agent in the cognitive and language performance of the students (Saif, 1985). ASL intervention refers to the processes by which an intervention agent such as a teacher, specialist or parent uses the sign language in interactions with deaf students to facilitate their communication and comprehension skills. It requires that the students attend to and analyze a set of syntactic structures that is different from English. However, it is beyond the scope of this article to discuss studies on deaf children's literacy skills in ASL, which completes the bridging process concerning ASL and English. For an in-depth discussion on sign language and reading and how a transition to English literacy is best achieved, readers are referred to Supalla et al. (2017). These scholars have proposed that a special written form of ASL that is hybridized with English will help systematize the teaching process with deaf children. The much needed comparative analysis lessons for ASL and English are contingent on these children having read in ASL and being able to bridge it to English.

Hearing students

The benefits of ASL for hearing students are predicated on the students' perceptual processing strategies to learn and use languages. Students vary in their perceptual processing schemata (Dunn, 1983) and preferred modalities for coding and processing information (McDonald, Teder-Sälejärvi, & Ward, 2001). Some students rely on visual processing strategies to learn languages, while other students rely on auditory processing strategies to learn languages, and still others rely on kinesthetic processing strategies (Barbe & Swassing, 1979). Rosen (2015) conducted a study of the perceptual processing schematas of speaking and hearing students of ASL. The students were asked about their perceptual processing schemata and how these affect their learning of ASL. It was found that students varied in their perceptual processing schemata. When they first learned signs and grammar, some of the students reported that they thought in pictures and images, other students reported that they thought in actions, and a few of the students depended on English translations. The bulk of the student responses demonstrated a preference for visual processing strategies. Apparently, ASL appeals to speaking and hearing students who largely rely on visual processing strategies to learn.

There are multiple motivations for hearing students to learn ASL. In the same study by Rosen (2015) on high school students who take ASL for foreign language credit, it was found that more than half of the students take sign language because they want to learn about deaf people and want to work with deaf people in the future, and/or that they want to teach the language in the future. Half of the students take ASL because they need to communicate with family and friends. For some hearing students, learning ASL will help students learn English better. About a third of the students take ASL because they failed other spoken foreign languages, which may be associated with their learning styles, as discussed earlier. This last finding suggests that ASL provides the students opportunities for completing the higher education degree by meeting a foreign language requirement for graduation that they might not meet otherwise.

One particular motivation among hearing students for learning ASL has to do with deaf students themselves, according to Rosen's 2015 study. In regular public schools where deaf students attend alongside hearing students, some hearing students have chosen ASL to communicate with their deaf classmates. This helps bolster communication between the students, and prevents mainstreamed deaf students from feeling isolated at their schools. For the hearing students, classes in ASL focus their awareness on deaf community and culture. Applying that knowledge through signing with deaf students appears to be fulfilling for the hearing students.

Finally, the extra-curricular uses of ASL as a foreign language by students of ASL demands attention. Rosen (2015) found certain interpersonal situations and social contexts that fostered the use of ASL in daily life. The interpersonal situations were created by the learners to use ASL instead of spoken English when they wanted to bond, tell secrets, express themselves with other learners and avoid having other people overhear their conversations. There were also social contexts that made it difficult for the learners to use spoken English and forced them to use visual-gestural languages such as ASL. These included locations that are noisy or quiet, or those with great distances between individuals who wish to communicate.

Quality Assurance: Challenges and Issues

While the benefits of ASL for deaf and hearing students may be great, the overall quality of how sign language is introduced remains an important consideration. This consideration leads to an outlining of some of the challenges and issues regarding L1 and L2/Ln teacher development and curriculum, instruction, and assessment.

Families and Schools with Deaf Children

Recall that many deaf children are born into a non-signing environment with hearing parents. This poses a challenge all its own. Had American society been both spoken and signed as reported for Martha's Vineyard, the situation of deaf children and their families with hearing parents would be radically different. According to various studies on the demographics of the deaf student population, about 92% of deaf children are born to hearing parents who do not sign at least initially, and 8% have deaf parents (Gallaudet Research Institute, 2013; Mitchell & Karchmer, 2005). According to Gallaudet Research Institute (GRI), 23% of family members regularly sign and close to 72% of the families do not sign (Gallaudet Research Institute, 2013). Statistics compiled by the GRI showed that their deaf parents tended to communicate in sign language with their deaf children. This is understandable given that deaf individuals would most likely be signers themselves. The fact that hearing parents tend not to communicate in ASL with their deaf children is troubling. With spoken language predominant in society, hearing parents who find their child is deaf face the task of learning ASL as a new language, and using it in the home in addition to the spoken language already in use.

The integration of deaf children in local public schools is a priority for society, as evident by the Individuals with Disabilities Education Act (IDEA), and complicates the language accessibility issues. An overwhelming majority, about 85 per cent, of deaf children have gone to mainstream programs instead of attending schools for the deaf (Shaver, Marschark, Newman, & Marder, 2014). Placed in a local public school where spoken language or English is used has ramifications for the children. Special education's emphasis on integration creates unintended consequences that undermine deaf children's access to ASL. Reports of poor sign language competency among integrated deaf students (e.g., Maller, Singleton, Supalla, & Wix, 1999; Padden & Ramsey, 2000) are understandable given that local public schools center on speaking, not signing.

According to J. H. Cripps and S. Supalla (2012), the push for deaf children's integration in speaking schools comes with a heavy price. The common provision of a sign language interpreter cannot be seen as good practice. As discussed earlier, deaf students need to undergo a bridging process from ASL to English literacy, which can be addressed in a signing school. It is reasonable to assume that only a school for the deaf has the capacity to see that deaf students be fluent readers of English, for instance. J. H. Cripps and S. Supalla explained that what it takes to teach literacy to deaf students would simply overwhelm a local public school. Deaf students are entitled to a signing teacher as much as hearing students are entitled to a speaking teacher. If one comes to visit a school for the deaf, the signing environment prevails and is frequently a rich one. Teachers and other staff are expected to sign throughout the entire day. Deaf teachers are widely known for being employed in deaf schools along with hearing teachers who sign, which helps provide strong language modeling for ASL acquisition.

When looking back at the history of deaf education, oralism can be viewed as a poorly conceived idea. In the past, many educators tried to make deaf children become speakers, while modern educators have a somewhat different view. However, the same underlying notion persists with the push towards promoting integration in the education system. Once again, educators are placing deaf children in a school environment with speakers. The assimilationist attitudes prevalent in special education are not sensitive to deaf students' differential needs. The American deaf community has protested over the integration practices as described, but they were shunned and put aside (Van Cleve, 1993). While special education is known for trying to address the needs of children with disabilities, it has to be done in a real and meaningful way. Signing and sign language are a serious business, greatly affecting the education of deaf students, especially in relation to linguistic accessibility (S. Supalla & J. H. Cripps, 2008).

When denied access to ASL, deaf children have experienced chronic underachievement in cognitive and literacy skills. This includes deprivation of linguistic and cognitive resources when these children do not have an opportunity for immersion in sign language (Schick et al., 2007; cf. Humphries et al., 2012). Deaf children with hearing parents are at risk. Being enrolled in a speaking school clearly will not help with this situation. The impact of language delay is particularly acute in the area of theory-of-mind abilities (Schick et al., 2007).

Schools for the deaf have a long way to go in terms of provisions for strong programming for deaf children. Unfortunately, a connection between ASL and English has not yet been pursued in a systematic way in any school for the deaf. Those with cochlear implants will need to be part of the same programming as they continue to be deaf and must participate in an education approach that works for them. Such reasoning is based on the understanding that deaf children with implants experience reading difficulties, and their reading performance worsens as they get older (Marschark, Sarchet, Rhoten, & Zupen, 2010).

A most fundamental need for deaf children is to have a legal mandate that will mandate their access to a well-established sign language such as ASL. The Education of the Deaf Act (EDA) enacted at the federal level does not include this mandate (S. Supalla, 1994). A significant amount of work will need to be done to improve this legislation as a part of The Higher Education Opportunity Act in 2008. Amending EDA is not a new idea as it has already undergone changes through the years as did IDEA. IDEA is designed for students with disabilities, whereas EDA is specifically for deaf children. The changes to EDA will align it to IDEA so that the two pieces of legislation will complement each other. Some new key provisions to EDA would require schools for the deaf to have highly qualified teachers from Pre-K through 12th grade. These schools will need to have a strong program for making sure that hearing parents who have deaf children are supported in their learning and use of ASL at home.

A more effective integration model could be pursued through EDA, which would encourage hearing siblings of deaf children and others who know ASL to enroll in a school for the deaf. This "reverse integration" is already taking place in a number of charter schools nationwide (Leigh, Andrews, & Harris, 2017). This innovative integration approach, among other practices, could help boost the status of schools for the deaf in the eyes of society. The reform as described here calls for re-inventing deaf education and turning it into a form of sign language education (J. H. Cripps & S. Supalla, 2012; Padden & Rayman, 2002). The new model would be more in tune with what is understood about linguistic accessibility and how to best teach deaf children.

Currently, deaf education appears to be declining with its future in question. Dolman (2010) studied student enrollment in teacher preparation programs in deaf education from 1973 to 2009. The number of programs increased from 65 in 1973 to a high of 81 in 1985, which has subsequently declined to 65 as of 2009. There were also decreasing number of teacher graduates; in 2009 there were about half of the number of graduates, 737, as compared to 1973 when 1,365 teachers graduated. Challenges to the deaf education programs came in the form of increased integration of deaf children in public schools, which brought different sets of requirements and expectations, and created connections with certain professions. For instance, there were increases in programs for interpreters (Dolman, 2010). Lenihan (2010) reported that several school districts have hired speech language pathologists to teach deaf children when they cannot find deaf-education-trained teachers. Whether all of the above-mentioned programs are competing for the same students has not been ascertained in Dolman's (2010) and Lenihan's (2010) studies.

Teacher of the deaf training programs that are ambiguous regarding ASL are especially problematic. For instance, Lenihan (2010) found that of about 65 deaf education teacher preparatory programs in 2009, 11 programs focused on listening and spoken languages, and 54 programs focused on visual communication strategies for teaching and learning academic subjects. Most teacher preparatory programs provide visual communication strategies for teachers to use in classrooms. However, whether these techniques promote higher literacy skills of ASL-using deaf children remains to be seen. Johnson (2004) in his review of past studies pointed to the tie between deaf student achievement and instructional effectiveness of teachers. This researcher noted that deaf children typically demonstrated sub-par literacy skills, which calls for attention to teacher training. Moreover, confusion within the schools and teacher preparatory programs about language and literacy issues is not a good trait for any profession. Sign language education needs to be put in the forefront in deaf education programs and at schools for the deaf nationwide. This will pave deaf students' way for effective learning. This would also help re-affirm the dissemination of ASL, as well as the continued maintenance of ASL as a standardized sign language, throughout the country.

Teaching ASL as L2/Ln

With the increased growth of classes in ASL in high schools, colleges, and universities, questions have been raised about what the ideal characteristics of an ASL teacher are, in particular, the knowledge, qualifications, and preparation of teachers of ASL as an L2/Ln language. Rosen (2008) conducted studies of L2 ASL public high school teachers and their preparation and qualifications. He found that teachers generally lack knowledge of L2/Ln research studies. He also found an insufficient number of certified and skilled teachers of L2 ASL. Regarding their degrees and certifications, nationally, a little more than a third of them earned a bachelor's degree as their highest degree, and half of them earned a master's degree as their highest degree. About a tenth of the teachers did not possess a collegiate degree. The highest degrees were in either deafness- or disability-related fields, with a few in the field of ASL teaching.

There are various areas of teacher certification held by teachers of ASL according to Rosen's 2008 study. Eighty percent of the teachers held more than one certification. Most (35%) of the ASL teachers held certification in deaf education, followed by ASL teaching (13%), K-12 general education (11%), and in fields other than deafness- or disability-related (8%). Five percent of the ASL teachers earned certificates from interpreter training programs. Six percent of the teachers possessed one of three levels of ASL instructor certification (provisional, qualified, and professional), based on degrees earned, experiences teaching ASL, workshops attended, and development of lesson plans, from the American Sign Language Teachers Association (ASLTA, 2016), a leading national credentialing organization of teachers of ASL. The teachers also varied in completed coursework and workshops. Nationally, most teachers took courses in deaf community and culture, but less than a half of the teachers took courses in the linguistics of ASL, second language acquisition, and methods and materials at credit-bearing colleges and universities. In addition, most teachers took non-credit-bearing workshops, which were often given at ASLTA conferences, in Deaf and ASL arts and literature, second language acquisition, and methods and materials in teaching ASL. The Rosen study includes anecdotal evidence that pointed to variations in signing quality among ASL teachers.

Regarding teachers of ASL in higher education institutions, there is little information on teacher preparation and qualifications. Cooper, Reisman, & Watson (2008) only provided the highest degree that was received by teachers of ASL. Cooper et al. (2008) reported that as of 2004, 11.6% of the ASL teachers possessed an associate degree, 34.2% held a bachelor's degree, 46.1% held a master's degree, and 8.1% held a doctoral degree. Newell (1995a) looked into the degrees and years of experience and whether they held certification from ASLTA. However, this study provided figures for all ASL teachers regardless of whether they teach in high schools or in colleges and universities. There are studies on desired, but not actual, skills and qualifications for ASL teachers such as by Newell (1995b) and Cooper et al. (2008, 2011). However, this information is beyond the scope of this section.

The discussion in this section has focused on ASL teaching in the classrooms of deaf and hearing students. Very little information is available on how hearing parents with deaf children are provided with sign language services. Home visits are a common feature for helping parents cope with the changes taking place in their homes, but how ASL teaching can be integrated into the home visits is not known. Anecdotally, some hearing parents take sign language classes at local colleges and universities, for instance, but there is no known study following their progress in becoming fluent signers. There are also some questions about how suitable the conventional ASL classes are for these parents. The parents would want to learn and use ASL, particularly in vocabulary and conversational grammar, for use with their deaf children. It is not clear whether the parents find attending conventional ASL classes to be satisfactory concerning their needs for parenting and communicating with their deaf children.

Curriculum and Instruction

The impact of training and quality control for teachers working with deaf and hearing students is examined here. Both curriculum and instructional concerns can be applied to the teaching of ASL as a language.

Curriculum for ASL as a first language. The curricular materials that are used by teachers of the deaf who use ASL in classrooms at schools for the deaf are predicated by the standards and requirements established by state education departments and local school districts. They cover academic subjects such as English literacy, math, science, and social studies. Unfortunately, in contrast to the offering of English at schools of the deaf, few schools for the deaf provide ASL as an academic subject for deaf children. Part of this can be attributed to how teachers typically focus on English even though ASL needs to be included in the picture, especially in terms of establishing a connection between the two languages.

Some schools for the deaf have begun to address the issue of ASL proficiency among deaf children. ASL intervention is used to identify and resolve difficulties, which may include review of sign vocabulary, structure and comprehension (Snoddon, 2008). There is a need for well-trained professionals that will not only address but also execute ASL intervention. Pathology in sign language production needs to be formally assessed to help combat the language deprivation situation faced by deaf children (J. H. Cripps, Cooper, S. Supalla, & Evitts, 2016). ASL intervention is currently provided by ASL specialists who are also teachers of the deaf. ASL specialists give assistance in class work with students and use ASL as a mediating, intervening language in enabling the students to comprehend the subject matter. As mentioned earlier, teacher preparation programs are ambiguous regarding ASL, and this is a serious concern. The fact that some ASL specialists offer classes in ASL for parents of deaf children is welcome, yet questionable in terms of professional knowledge and background.

Curriculum for ASL as a second or additional language. At first glance, the curricular materials that are used by teachers of ASL as L2/L*n* are multiple and impressive. Such materials include: *A Basic Course in American Sign Language* (Humphries, Padden, & O'Rourke, 1994); *The American Sign Language Phrase Book* (Fant, 1983); *Bravo* (Cassell, 1997); *Learning American Sign Language Levels I and II* (Humphries & Padden, 2004); *Green Books: American Sign Language: Teacher's Resource on Curriculum, Grammar and Culture* and *Student Text* (Cokely & Baker-Shenk, 1980a-e); The *Vista American Sign Language Series: Signing Naturally* (Lentz, Mikos, & Smith, 2001, 2014; Mikos, Smith, Lentz, 2001; Smith, Lentz, & Mikos, 2008); and *Master ASL!* (Zinza, 2006). Each curriculum includes certain assumptions about language, teaching, and learning that are influenced by the prevailing theories and approaches in linguistics, the psychology of learning and teaching, and a value system for topics. In addition, curricula vary in emphasis on cultural information on the use of language in different social situations and with various persons, and the historical, political, economic, and social characteristics of the community.

In spite of curricular availability, the questionable quality of training for ASL teachers as discussed earlier continues to be a problem. According to Rosen (2015), ASL teachers do not have a strong understanding of the theoretical, empirical, and pedagogical assumptions the various curricula have about L2 teaching and learning. Each of the ASL curricula rest on a variety of linguistic, learning, and pedagogical assumptions, which have transformed over time. Some teachers used ASL curricula that subscribe to older assumptions, while other teachers used ASL curricula subscribing to recent assumptions. There are inconsistencies in curricula used by teachers of ASL. Pedagogical practices are often created by 'gut' feelings, not scholarly, systematic understanding of what curriculum is, and what teaching entails. Inconsistencies in the selection of curricula used by L2 ASL teachers raises questions about the understanding of the teachers of the principles and practices in second language curriculum development and instructional strategies. The teachers need to understand the assumptions that guide the development of curriculum. More specifically, teachers need to acknowledge that curricula differ in the selection of topics, types of linguistic structures, and the degree of emphasis on vocabulary, grammar, and culture information in teaching and learning.

The fact that many ASL teachers are deaf themselves (Cooper et al., 2008; Newell, 1995a,b) must be applauded for bringing authenticity to the learning experience of hearing students. These students find themselves not only learning a new language, but also having direct contact with those who use sign language as their primary language. One still wonders if deaf teachers' own education plays a role in the present situation of how the metalinguistic awareness related to ASL needs improvement. Deaf people as a group are known for being signers over the years, but their knowledge about their own language, ASL is frequently limited. The situation of hearing students who are themselves excluded from enrolling in a school for the deaf and thus miss the opportunity for immersion in ASL has ramifications as well. Only recently has Gallaudet University opened its enrollment to hearing undergraduates (Behm, 2010; de Vise, 2011). Along with the needed changes to how deaf education is set up, such changes point to future directions for educators and policymakers.

Closing Remarks

This review of studies on access to, benefits of, and delivery quality in ASL reveal areas of accomplishments, concerns and promise. There is access to ASL in the American education system that can be improved in various areas. With remarkably rapid growth, offering ASL programs and classes serves as a testament to both the efforts of members of the deaf community and society's increasing acceptance for sign language as a human language. What needs to be addressed in the future is the prospect of all hearing students having the opportunity to learn ASL, and not just for meeting the foreign language requirement. This would be part of fulfilling a universal design concept, where an entire society knows and communicates via an alternative language system such as ASL (S. Supalla, Small, & J. S. Cripps, 2013). The idea that all hearing students study ASL as they do English, math, science, and social studies is bold, yet beneficial. Future studies should examine how learning ASL shapes the architecture of spatial working memory within and outside the linguistic domain among hearing learners and users. Any cognitive boost for hearing learners, as was reported for deaf learners, would be welcome in a society that supports stronger cognitive functioning for its citizens, for instance.

What must be recognized here is the disparity between hearing and deaf children in language development. The former are experiencing increasing access to ASL, while the latter continue to suffer from a lack of attention to sign language-based curriculum, instruction, and assessment and the persistence of spoken language bias in education and society. The polarity and social injustice as described here should not be tolerated. ASL owes its origins to deaf people themselves, but society must be held accountable for its signing citizens and be fully supportive of sign language. This requires sign language planning that ensures benefits and successful outcomes for all American citizens. Both L1 and L2/Ln considerations and the professionalization of sign language education, are crucial to such planning. This will occur when inclusiveness and diversity are accepted practices in society so that deaf people are recognized as a part of the variegation of human life, and ASL as a natural, human language.

References

Ausbrooks, M. (2007). *Predictors of reading success among deaf bilinguals: Examining the relationship between American Sign Language and English*. Unpublished manuscript, Lamar University, Beaumont, TX.

Bahan, B., & Poole-Nash, J. C. (1996). The formation of signing communities. In V. Walter (Ed.), *Deaf studies IV: Visions of the past, visions for the future* (pp. 1-26). Washington, DC: College for Continuing Education, Gallaudet University.

Barbe, W. B., & Swassing, R. H. (1979). *Teaching through modality strengths: Concepts and practices*. Columbus, OH: Zaner-Bloser.

Bauman, H. D. L. (2004). Exploring the metaphysics of oppression. *Journal of Deaf Studies and Deaf Education, 9*(2), 239-246.

Bavelier, D., Tomann, A., Hutton, C., Mitchell, T., Corina, D., Liu, G., & Neville, H. (2000). Visual attention to the periphery is enhanced in congenitally deaf individuals. *The Journal of Neuroscience, 20*, 1-6.

Baynton, D. C. (1996). *Forbidden signs: American culture and the campaign against sign language*. Chicago, IL: The University of Chicago Press.

Behm, D. (2010, November 26). This is Gallaudet. *The Buff and Blue – Lifestyle*. Retrieved from http://www.thebuffandblue.net/?p=4452

Bettiger, J., Emmorey, K., McCullough, S., & Bellugi, U. (1997). Facial processing: The influence of American Sign Language experience. *Journal of Deaf Studies and Deaf Education, 2*(4), 223-233.

Boudreault, P., & Mayberry, R. I. (2006). Grammatical processing in American Sign Language: Age of acquisition effects in relation to syntactic structure. *Language and Cognitive Processes, 21*(5), 608-635.

Cassell, J. (1997). *Bravo! ASL curriculum*. Salem, OR: Sign Enhancers.

Center for Applied Linguistics. (1997). *A national survey of foreign language instruction in elementary and high schools: A changing picture: 1987–1997*. Washington, DC: Author.

Chamberlain, C., & Mayberry, R. I. (2000). Theorizing about the relation between ASL and reading. In C. Chamberlain, J. P. Morford, & R. I. Mayberry (Eds.), *Language acquisition by eye* (pp. 221-259). Mahwah, NJ: Lawrence Erlbaum.

Christensen, J. B., & Barnartt, S. N. (2003). *Deaf president now!: The 1988 revolution at Gallaudet University*. Washington, DC: Gallaudet University Press.

Codina, C., Buckley, D., Port, M., & Pascalis, O. (2011) Deaf and hearing children: A comparison of peripheral vision development. *Developmental Science, 14*(4), 725-737.

Cokely, D., & Baker-Shenk, C. (1980a). *American Sign Language: A student's text, units 1–9*. Washington, DC: Gallaudet College Press.

Cokely, D., & Baker-Shenk, C. (1980b). *American Sign Language: A student's text, units 10–18*. Washington, DC: Gallaudet College Press.

Cokely, D., & Baker-Shenk, C. (1980c). *American Sign Language: A student's text, units 19–27.* Washington, DC: Gallaudet College Press.

Cokely, D., & Baker-Shenk, C. (1980d). *American Sign Language: A teacher's resource text on curriculum, methods, and evaluation.* Washington, DC: Gallaudet College Press.

Cokely, D., & Baker-Shenk, C. (1980e). *American Sign Language: A teacher's resource text on grammar and culture.* Washington, DC: Gallaudet College Press.

Cooper, S. (1997). *The academic status of sign language programs in institutions of higher education in the United States* (Unpublished doctoral dissertation). Gallaudet University, Washington, DC.

Cooper, S. B., Reisman, J. I., & Watson, D. (2008). The status of sign language instruction in institutions of higher education: 1994-2004. *American Annals of the Deaf, 153*(1), 78-88.

Cooper, S. B., Reisman, J. I., & Watson, D. (2011). Sign language program structure and content in institutions of higher education in the United States, 1994-2004. *Sign Language Studies, 11*(3), 298-328.

Corwin, K., & Wilcox, S. (1985). The search for the empty cup continues. *Sign Language Studies, 48*, 249–268.

Cripps, J. H., Cooper, S. B., Supalla, S. J., & Evitts, P. M. (2016). Meeting the needs of signers in the field of speech and language pathology: Some considerations for action. *Communication Disorders Quarterly, 37*(2), 108-116.

Cripps, J. H., & Supalla, S. J. (2012). The power of spoken language in schools and deaf students who sign. *International Journal of Humanities and Social Science, 2*(16), 86-102.

Davis, L. (1998). The linguistic turf battles over American Sign Language. *The Chronicle of Higher Education, 44*, 60–64.

De Garcia, B. G. (2003). Acquisition of English literacy by signing deaf children. *Ponto de Vista Florianopolis, 5*, 129-150.

Delgado, G. L. (1984). A survey of sign language instruction in junior and community colleges. *American Annals of the Deaf, 129*(1), 38-39.

De Vise, D. (2011, September 24). Gallaudet University adjusts to a culture that includes more hearing students. *The Washington Post.* Retrieved from https://www.washingtonpost.com/local/education/gallaudet-university-adjusts-to-a-culture-that-includes-more-hearing-students/2011/09/23/gIQAC3W9tK_story.html?utm_term=.77fc7163ff39

Dolman, D. (2010). Enrollment trends in deaf education teacher preparation programs, 1973-2009. *American Annals of the Deaf, 155*(3), 353-359.

Dunn, R. (1983). Learning style and its relation to exceptionality at both ends of the spectrum. *Exceptional Children, 49*, 496-506.

Eckert, R. C., & Rowley, A. J. (2013). Audism: A theory and practice of audio centric privilege. *Humanity & Society, 37*(2), 101-130.

Edwards, L., Figueras, B., Mellanby, J., & Langdon, D. (2011). Verbal and spatial analogical reasoning in deaf and hearing children: The role of grammar and vocabulary. *Journal of Deaf Studies and Deaf Education, 16*(2), 189-197.

Ellis, R. (2003). *Task-based language learning and teaching.* New York, NY: Oxford University Press.

Emmorey, K. (2002). *Language, cognition, and the brain: Insights from sign language research.* Mahwah, NJ: Lawrence Erlbaum and Associates.

Emmorey, K., Corina, D., & Bellugi, U. (1995). Differential processing of topographic and referential functions of space. In K. Emmorey & J. S. Reilly (Eds.), *Language, gesture, and space* (pp. 43-62). Mahwah, NJ: Lawrence Erlbaum Associates.

Emmorey, K., Kosslyn, S. M., & Bellugi, U. (1993). Visual imagery and visual-spatial language: Enhanced imagery abilities in deaf and hearing ASL signers. *Cognition, 46*, 139-181.

Erting, C., & Kuntze, M. (2008). Language socialization in deaf communities. In P. A. Duff & N. H. Hornberger (Eds.), *Encyclopedia of language and education* (2nd ed., Vol. 8, pp. 287-300). New York, NY: Springer Publishing.

Fant, L. (1983). *The American Sign Language phrase book.* Lincolnwood, IL: Contemporary Books.

Fischer, S., & Siple, P. (1990). *Theoretical issues in sign language research.* Chicago, IL: The University of Chicago Press.

Foster, S. (1989). Social alienation and peer identification: A study of the social construction of deafness. *Human Organization, 48*, 226–235.

Frishberg, N. (1988). Signers of tales: The case for literary status of an unwritten language. *Sign Language Studies, 59*, 149–170.

Fromkin, V. A. (1988). Sign language: Evidence for language universals and the linguistic capacity of the human brain. *Sign Language Studies, 59*, 115–128.

Gallaudet Research Institute. (2004). *States that recognize American Sign Language as a foreign language.* Retrieved from http://clerccenter.gallaudet.edu/InfoToGo/index.html

Gallaudet Research Institute. (2013). *Regional and national summary report of data from the*

2011-12 annual survey of deaf and hard of hearing children and youth. Washington, DC: Gallaudet University.

Gaustad, M. G., & Kluwin, T. N. (1992). Patterns of communication among deaf and hearing adolescents. In T. N. Kluwin, D. F. Moores, & M. G. Gaustad (Eds.), *Toward effective school programs for deaf students* (pp. 107-128). New York, NY: Teachers College Press.

Goldberg, D., Looney, D., & Lusin, N. (2015). *Enrollments in languages other than English in United States institutions of higher education: Fall 2013.* New York, NY: Modern Language Association.

Groce, N. (1985). *Everyone here spoke sign language: Hereditary deafness on Martha's Vineyard.* Cambridge, MA: Harvard University Press.

Grushkin, D. A. (2017). Writing signed languages: What for? What form? *American Annals of the Deaf, 161*(5), 509-527.

Hauser, P. C., Cohen, J., Dye, M. W., & Bavelier, D. (2007). Visual constructive and visual-motor skills in deaf native signers. *Journal of Deaf Studies and Deaf Education, 12*(2), 148-57.

Hawkins, R. (2001). *Second language syntax: A generative introduction.* Oxford, UK: Blackwell Publishers, Ltd.

Higher Education Opportunity Act, Pub. L. 110-315, 122 Stat. 3450. (2008). Retrieved from https://www.gpo.gov/fdsys/pkg/PLAW-110publ315/pdf/PLAW-110publ315.pdf

Hoffmeister, R., Philip, M., Costello, P., & Grass, W. (1997). Evaluating American Sign Language in deaf children: ASL influences own reading with a focus on classifiers, plurals, verbs of motion and location. In J. Mann (Ed.), *Proceedings of deaf studies V conference* (pp. 22-31). Washington, DC: Gallaudet University.

Hoffmeister, R. J. (2000). A piece of the puzzle: ASL and reading comprehension in deaf children. In C. Chamberlain, J. P. Morford, & R. Mayberry (Eds.), *Language acquisition by eye* (pp. 143-163). Mahwah, NJ: Lawrence Erlbaum Publishers.

Hoffmeister, R. J., & Caldwell-Harris, C. L. (2014). Acquiring English as a second language via print: The task for deaf children. *Cognition, 132*(2), 229-242.

Hopkins, J. (2008). Choosing how to write sign language: A sociolinguistic perspective. *International Journal of the Sociology of Language, 192*, 75-89.

Humphries, T., Kushalnagar, P., Mathur, G., Napoliu, D. J., Padden, C., Rathmann, C., & Smith, S. R. (2012). Language acquisition for deaf children: Reducing the harms of zero tolerance to the use of alternative approaches. *Harm Education Journal, 9*(16), 1-9.

Humphries, T., & Padden, C. (2004). *Learning American Sign Language: Levels I and II* (2nd ed.). San Francisco, CA: Holt, Rinehart, and Winston.

Humphries, T., Padden, C., & O'Rourke, T. (1994). *A basic course in American Sign Language* (2nd ed.). Silver Spring, MD: Linstok.

Jacobowitz, E. L. (1999, October 7-10). *American Sign Language in higher education: Implications for administrators and teacher trainers.* Paper presented at the American Sign Language Teachers Association – Professional Development Conference, Rochester, NY.

Jarvis, S., & Pavlenko, A. (2008). *Crosslinguistic influence in language and cognition.* New York, NY: Routledge.

Johnson, H. A. (2004). U.S. deaf education teacher preparation programs: A look at the present and a vision for the future. *American Annals of the Deaf, 149*(2), 75-91.

Johnson, R. E., Liddell, S. K., & Erting, C. J. (1989). *Unlocking the curriculum: Principles for achieving access in deaf education* (Gallaudet Research Institute Working/Occasional Paper Series, No. 89-3). Washington, DC: Gallaudet Research Institute.

Klima, E., & Bellugi, U. (1979). *The signs of language.* Cambridge, MA: Harvard University Press.

Kreeft-Peyton, J. (1998). ASL as a foreign language. *K-12 Foreign Language Education, 6*, 1–3.

Kuntze, M. (2004). *Literacy acquisition and deaf children: A study of the interaction between ASL and written English* (Unpublished dissertation). Stanford University, Stanford, CA.

Lane, H. L. (1992). *The mask of benevolence: Disabling the deaf community.* New York, NY: Alfred A. Knopf, Inc.

Langacker, R. W. (1987). *Foundations of cognitive grammar: Theoretical perspectives* (Vol. 1). Palo Alto, CA: Stanford University Press.

Leigh, I. W., Andrews, J. F., & Harris, R. L. (2017). *Deaf culture: Exploring deaf communities in the United States.* San Diego, CA: Plural Publishing.

Lenihan, S. (2010). Trends and challenges in teacher preparation in deaf education. *The Volta Review, 110*(2), 117-128.

Lentz, E. M., Mikos, K., & Smith, C. (2001). *Signing naturally: Teacher's curriculum guide: Level 2.* San Diego, CA: DawnSignPress.

Lentz, E. M., Mikos, K., & Smith, C. (2014). *Signing naturally: Teacher's curriculum guide: Units 7-12*. San Diego, CA: DawnSignPress.

Liddell, S. K. (1980). *American Sign Language syntax*. The Hague, NL: Mouton Publishers.

Lillo-Martin, D. (2000). Early and late in language acquisition: Aspects of the syntax and acquisition wh-questions in American Sign Language. In K. Emmorey & H. Lane (Eds.), *The signs of language revisited: An anthology to honor Ursula Bellugi and Edward Klima* (pp. 401-414). Mahwah, NJ: Lawrence Erlbaum Associates.

Lillo-Martin, D., & Pichler, D. C. (2006). Acquisition of syntax in signed languages. In B. Schick, M. Marschark, & P. E. Spencer (Eds.), *Advances in the sign language development of deaf children* (pp. 231-261). New York, NY: Oxford University Press.

Maller, S. J., Singleton, J. L., Supalla, S. J., & Wix, T. (1999). The development and psychometric properties of the American Sign Language Proficiency Assessment (ASL-PA). *Journal of Deaf Studies and Deaf Education, 4*(4), 249-269.

Marschark, M., Sarchet, T., Rhoten, C., & Zupen, M. (2010). Will cochlear implants close the reading achievement gap for deaf students? In M. Marschark & P. E. Spencer (Eds.), The Oxford handbook of deaf studies, language, and education (Vol. 2, pp. 127-143). Oxford, UK: Oxford University Press.

Mayberry, R. I., del Giudice, A. A., & Lieberman, A. M. (2011). Reading achievement in relation to phonological coding and awareness in deaf readers: A meta-analysis. *Journal of Deaf Studies and Deaf Education, 16*(2), 164-188.

Mayberry, R. I., & Eichen, E. B. (1991). The long-lasting advantage of learning sign language in childhood: Another look at the critical period for language acquisition. *Journal of Memory and Language, 30,* 486–512.

McDonald, J. J., Teder-Sälejärvi, W. A., & Ward, L. M. (2001). Multisensory integration and cross-modal attention effects in the human brain. *Science, 292,* 1791.

McIntire, M. (1984). Achieving academic acceptance. *The Reflector: A Journal for Sign Language Teachers and Interpreters, 8,* 5-6.

Meier, R. P. (1991). Language acquisition by deaf children. *American Scientist, 79*(1), 60-70.

Meier, R. P., & Newport, E. L. (1990). Out of the hands of babies: On a possible sign advantage in language acquisition. *Language, 66*(1), 1-23.

Mikos, K., Smith, C., & Lentz, E. M. (2001). *Signing naturally: Teacher's curriculum guide: Level 3*. San Diego, CA: DawnSignPress.

Miller, C. (2001). Some reflections on the need for a common sign notation. *Sign Language & Lingusitcs, 4*(1/2), 11-28.

Mitchell, R. E., & Karchmer, M. A. (2005). Parental hearing status and signing among deaf and hard of hearing students. *Sign Language Studies, 5*(2), 231-244.

Neidle, C., Kegl, J., MacLaughlin, D., Bahan, B., & Lee, R. (2000). *The syntax of American Sign Language: Functional categories and hierarchical structure*. Cambridge, MA: MIT Press.

Newell, W. (1995a). A profile of professionals teaching American Sign Language. *Sign Language Studies, 86*, 19–36.

Newell, W. (1995b). American Sign Language teachers: Practices and perceptions. *Sign Language Studies, 87*, 141–165.

Newport, E. L. (1990). Maturational constraints on language learning. *Cognitive Science, 14*(1), 11-28.

Newport, E. L., & Meier, R. P. (1985). The acquisition of American Sign Language. In D. Slobin (Ed.), The cross-linguistic study of language acquisition (pp. 881-938). Hillside, NJ: Lawrence Erlbaum.

Nover, S., & Ruiz, R. (1992). ASL and language planning in deaf education. In D. Martin & R. Mobley (Eds.), *Proceedings of the first international symposium on teacher education in deafness* (pp. 153-171). Washington, DC: Gallaudet University Press.

Padden, C. (1981). Some arguments for syntactic patterning in American Sign Language. *Sign Language Studies, 32*, 239–259.

Padden, C. (2006) Learning fingerspelling twice: Young signing children's acquisition of fingerspelling. In M. Marschark, B. Schick, & P. Spencer (Eds.). *Advances in sign language development by deaf children* (pp. 189-201). New York, NY: Oxford University Press.

Padden, C., & Humphries, T. (1988). *Deaf in America: Voices from a culture*. Cambridge, MA: Harvard University Press.

Padden, C., & Humphries, T. (2005). *Inside deaf culture*. Cambridge, MA: Harvard University Press.

Padden, C., & Ramsey, C. (1998). Reading ability in signing deaf children. *Topics in Language Disorders, 18*(4), 30-46.

Padden, C., & Ramsey, C. (2000). American Sign Language and reading ability in deaf children. In C. Chamberlain, J. P. Morford, & R. Mayberry (Eds.), *Language acquisition by eye* (pp. 165-189). Mahwah, NJ: Lawrence Erlbaum Associates.

Padden, C., & Rayman, J. (2002). Concluding thoughts: The future of American Sign Language. In J. V. Van Cleve, D. F. Armstrong, & M. A. Karchmer (Eds.), *The study of signed languages: Essays in honor of William C. Stokoe* (pp. 247-261). Washington, DC: Gallaudet University Press.

Pettito, L. A. (1994). On the equipotentiality of signed and spoken language in early language ontogeny. In B. Snider (Ed.), *Post-Milan ASL and English literacy: Issues, trends, and research* (pp. 195-223). Washington, DC: Gallaudet College Press.

Pettito, L. A., Zatorre, R. J., Gauna, K., Nikelski, E. J., Dostie, D., & Evans, A. C. (2000). Speech-like cerebral activity in profoundly deaf people possessing signed languages: Implications for the neural basis of human language. *Proceedings of the National Academy of Sciences of the United States of America, 97*(25), 13961-13966.

Prinz, P., & Strong, M. (1998). ASL proficiency and English literacy within a bilingual deaf education model of instruction. *Topics in Language Disorders, 18*(4), 47-60.

Prinz, P., & Strong, M. (2000). Is American Sign Language skill related to English literacy? In C. Chamberlain, J. P. Morford, & R. Mayberry (Eds.), *Language acquisition by eye* (pp. 131-141). Mahwah, NJ: Lawrence Erlbaum Publishers.

Reilly, J., McIntire, M., & Bellugi, U. (1990). Conditionals in American Sign Language: Grammaticalized facial expressions. *Applied Psycholinguistics, 11*(4), 369-392.

Rosen, R. (2006). An unintended consequence of IDEA: American Sign Language, the deaf community, and deaf culture into mainstream education. *Disability Studies Quarterly, 26*(2). Retrieved from http://dsq-sds.org/article/view/685/862

Rosen, R. (2008). American Sign Language as a foreign language in US high schools: State of the art. *Modern Language Journal, 92*(1), 10-38.

Rosen, R. (2015). *Learning American Sign Language in high school: Motivation, strategies, and achievement*. Washington, DC: Gallaudet University Press.

Rosen, R. S., Hartman, M. C., & Wang, Y. (2017). "Thinking-For-Writing": A prolegomenon on writing signed languages. *American Annals of the Deaf, 161*(5), 528-536.

Rutherford, S. A. (1988). The culture of American deaf people. *Sign Language Studies, 59*, 129-148.

Saif, P. (1985). Analysis. In D. Martin (Ed.), *Cognition, education, and deafness* (pp. 196-200). Washington, DC: Gallaudet University Press.

Sandler, W., & Lillo-Martin, D. (2006). *Sign language and linguistic universals*. Cambridge, UK: Cambridge University Press.

Schick, B., De Villiers, P., De Villiers, J., & Hoffmeister, R. (2007). Language and theory of mind: A study of deaf children. *Child Development, 78*(2), 376-396.

Shaver, D. M., Marschark, M., Newman, L., & Marder, C. (2014). Who is where? Characteristics of deaf and hard of hearing students in regular and special schools. *Journal of Deaf Studies and Deaf Education, 19*(2), 203-219.

Shroyer, E. H., & Holmes, D. W. (1982). Sign students in sign language classes. *The Reflector: A Journal for Sign Language Teachers and Interpreters, 3*, 21–22.

Sign Course Inventory. (1984). *The Reflector: A Journal for Sign Language Teachers and Interpreters, 8*, 12-17.

Singleton, J. L., Supalla, S., Litchfield, S., & Schley, S. (1998). From sign to word: Considering modality constraints in ASL/English bilingual education. *Topics in Language Disorders, 18*(4), 16-29.

Sisco, F. H., & Anderson, R. J. (1980). Deaf children's performance on the WISC-R relative to hearing status of parents and child-rearing experiences. *American Annals of the Deaf, 125*, 923-930.

Smith, A. (2007). *The performance of deaf students on a test of American Sign Language abilities—Receptive (TASLA—R)* (Unpublished doctoral dissertation). Lamar University, Beaumont, TX.

Smith, C., Lentz, E. M., & Mikos, K. (2008). *Signing naturally: Teacher's curriculum guide: Units 1-6*. San Diego, CA: DawnSignPress.

Snoddon, K. (2008). American Sign Language and early intervention. *The Canadian Modern Language Review/La Revue Canadienne Des Langues Vivantes, 64*(4), 581-604.

Stinson, M. S., & Liu, Y. (1999). Participation of deaf and hard of hearing students in classes with hearing students. *Journal of Deaf Studies and Deaf Education, 4*(3), 191–202.

Stokoe, W. C. (1960). *Sign language structure: An outline of the visual communication system of the American deaf*. Washington, DC: Gallaudet College Press.

Stokoe, W. C., Casterline, D., & Croneberg, C. (1965). *A dictionary of American Sign Language on linguistic principles*. Washington, DC: Gallaudet College Press.

Supalla, S. J. (1994). Equality in educational opportunities: The deaf version. In C. J. Erting, R. C. Johnson, D. L. Smith, & B. D. Snider (Eds.), *The deaf way: Perspectives from the international conference on deaf culture* (pp. 584-592). Washington, DC: Gallaudet University Press.

Supalla, S. J., & Cripps, J. H. (2008). Linguistic accessibility and deaf children. In B. Spolsky & F. M. Hult (Eds.), *The handbook of educational linguistics* (pp. 174-191). Oxford, UK: Blackwell.

Supalla, S. J., Cripps, J. H., & Byrne, A. P. J. (2017). Why American Sign Language gloss must matter. *American Annals of the Deaf, 161*(5), 540-551.

Supalla, S. J., Small, A., & Cripps, J. S. (2013). *American Sign Language for everyone: Considerations for universal design and deaf youth identity* (Monograph Series 2). Toronto, ON: Canadian Cultural Society of the Deaf & Knowledge Network for Applied Educational Research.

Supalla, T., & Clark, P. (2014). *Sign language archaeology: Understanding the historical roots of American Sign Language*. Washington, DC: Gallaudet University Press.

Van Cleve, J. V. (1993). The academic integration of deaf children. In R. Fischer & H. Lane (Eds.), *A reader on the history of deaf communities and their sign languages* (pp. 333-347). Hamburg, DL: Signum Press.

Van Cleve, J. V., & Couch, B. A. (1989). *A place of their own: Creating the deaf community in America*. Washington, DC: Gallaudet University Press.

van der Hulst, H., & Channon, R. (2010). Notation systems. In D. Brentari (Ed.), *Sign languages* (pp. 151-172). Cambridge, UK: Cambridge University Press.

Wilbur, R. (1979). *American Sign Language and sign systems*. Baltimore, MD: University Park Press.

Wilbur, R. (2000). The use of ASL to support the development of English and literacy. *Journal of Deaf Studies and Deaf Education, 5*(1), 81-104.

Wilcox, S. (1992). *Academic acceptance of American Sign Language*. Burtonsville, MD: Linstok Press.

Wilcox, S. (2006). *Universities that accept ASL as a foreign language*. Retrieved from www.unm.edu/%7ewilcox/universities_that_accept_as.htm

Wilcox, S. (2015). *Universities that accept ASL as a foreign language*. Retrieved from www.unm.edu/%7ewilcox/universities_that_accept_as.htm

Wilcox, S., & Wilcox, P. (1991). *Learning to see: Teaching American Sign Language as a second language* (1st ed.). Washington, DC: Gallaudet University Press.

Williams, C. L. (1999). Preschool deaf children's use of signed language during writing events. *Journal of Literacy Research, 31*(2), 183-212.

Wilson, M., Bettiger, J. G., Niculae, I., & Klima, E. S. (1997). Modality of language shapes working memory: Evidence from digit span and spatial span in ASL signers. *Journal of Deaf Studies and Deaf Education, 2*(3), 123-132.

Zinza, J. E. (2006). *Master ASL! Level one.* Burtonsville, MD: Sign Media, Inc.

A Sketch on Reading Methodology for Deaf Children

Samuel J. Supalla
University of Arizona

Abstract

A well-established reading methodology is much needed in the field of deaf education. While the concept of signed language reading is intriguing and underappreciated, it has some of the clearest implications for how to teach reading to deaf children. This paper begins by covering historical attempts to have deaf children learn to read in signed language. The distinction between signed language reading and spoken language reading is part of the paper's creation of a cohesive theoretical basis outlining best reading instruction practices. A key element of the discussion is how deaf children find text readable when it represents the language that they know, American Sign Language (ASL). This includes utilizing glossing as an intermediary system and reading methodology which enable deaf children to experience a transition to English literacy, all the while learning to read in ASL. Some indications of signed language reading (associated with glossing) are laid out through a review of published research reports. Deaf children in a charter school setting are highlighted in a variety of reading behaviors resembling hearing learners in early elementary school years. Signed language reading incorporates parallel concepts such as sounds, phonics, phonemic awareness, reading-aloud, and sounding out. The paper's emphasis on the liberal application of key concepts for reading processes produces a scenario where deafness may no longer serve as a barrier to reading.

Introduction

Teaching deaf children how to read is highly desirable, yet elusive. With this paper, the focus is on understanding reading methodology and how it can help deaf children learn to read. Over the years, educators have debated language issues that are still relevant today. However, the primary function of a school is to teach reading and writing skills. Thus, to help redirect educators towards literacy with deaf children, a formal distinction between signed language reading and spoken language reading must be made. This begins a dialogue on how deaf children can best learn to read. Not only are American Sign Language (ASL) and English two distinct languages, they represent languages in two different modalities: signed vs. spoken (Singleton, S. Supalla, Litchfield, & Schley, 1998). Deaf children are known for being native signers and thinking and processing in signed language (Lane, Hoffmeister, & Bahan, 1996). This prevalence of signed language knowledge must be seen as an asset in considerations of reading pedagogy. This includes making ASL text a part of deaf children's reading development experiences.

With English, the reading situation is understandably problematic for deaf children as they do not hear the language in question. This is where spoken language reading has serious limitations. Children born profoundly deaf or becoming deaf before the age of two would not have the ability to internalize English and utilize the spoken language knowledge for reading development purposes. Descriptions of the experience of learning to read in English as bewildering for deaf children (Hoffmeister & Caldwell-Harris, 2014) is especially troubling. A child who can hear would have spoken language knowledge in place and use it as a reference point for learning to read English. In contrast, the deaf child does not have this type of knowledge to help with the reading process (Paul & Quigley, 1987; see Paul, 1994 for further discussion on the reading complications that arise for deaf children with English). In a typical classroom with deaf children in a school for the deaf, the print has been strictly limited to English. Yet these children know ASL, and thus written English is foreign and inaccessible.

With the provision of ASL text, deaf children integrate their knowledge with linguistic concepts, which is the most important principle for reading instruction. Reading then has the potential to become effective along a trajectory of teachable skills. Equally important is the prospect for deaf children to experience a transition to English literacy at the same time. Goldin-Meadow and Mayberry (2001) proposed that an intermediary system be developed for deaf children so that they could map ASL onto English literacy for optimal learning outcomes. While the intermediary system idea is novel and intriguing, details on what it might look like are lacking. This paper intends to detail an innovative reading instruction approach called glossing. Glossing is identified in this paper as the intermediary system that was implemented in a charter school in Arizona. ASL text is part of this framework along with other tools and procedures.

This represents an important difference from hearing children, as they normally learn to read in just one language. If they had to learn another language, they would repeat the reading process in ways similar to the first language. This reinforces the idea that "[second language or L2] proficiency is a vital prerequisite to efficient L2 reading," a statement by the L2 reading theorist, Keiko Koda (2005, p. 23). What this suggests is that deaf children must learn spoken English in order to read it effectively. This is clearly unfair due to their disability. It is clear that the established reading theories account for one language mapping only for monolingualism and bilingualism (e.g., Adams, 1990; Grabe, 2009; Hoover & Gough, 1990; Koda, 2005; Snow, Burns, & Griffin, 1998). As discussed in S. Supalla and Cripps (2011), hearing children do not use one language to decode another language (based on current reading methodologies), but this is precisely what deaf children are required to do. Glossing, a cross-linguistic reading instruction approach, provides insights and methodological details for improving this situation.

A review of research literature on glossing will follow, emphasizing a variety of ASL reading behaviors that deaf children at the Arizona charter school modeled, and a comparison to what is known for spoken language reading. To help create a strong sense of background on signed language reading, the paper will begin with a discussion of efforts occurring in the early nineteenth century. Perhaps a surprise to many in the field of deaf education, signed language reading was actively pursued at that time. However, readers will learn that a different signed language reading model was pursued instead of glossing. Coverage of previous efforts will point to the strengths of glossing as a reading methodology for deaf children.

Early Attempts with Signed Language Reading

At the time of writing this paper, American deaf education has reached its 200-year mark, but the field has a longer history, considering that the world's first public school for the deaf was founded in Paris, France. This school served as a model for many nations worldwide, including the United States (Van Cleve & Crouch, 1989). At the Paris school for the deaf, the concept of signed language reading was first explored. However, the French educators were largely occupied with language issues before shifting their attention to reading issues. This is understandable as reading is contingent on language. The important question raised at the time was whether signing should approximate the structure of French or best stood as a distinctive language. When the school was opened, a signed version of French was developed and used with deaf children. Knowing French through the signed medium was thought to help deaf children with learning to read in French (see Mayer & Wells, 1996 for a similar assumption concerning signed English as used in the United States and Canada). However, through the test of time educators came to the conclusion that Natural Sign (the name they gave to the communication system that deaf children used among themselves) was the better choice (see S. Supalla & McKee, 2002 for a psycholinguistic explanation on why a sign system modeling the structure of a spoken language is ill-advised and problematic). Although Natural Sign was not French, the idea of deaf children using a language that worked for them superseded the educators' intention of confining deaf education to the French language.

French educator, Roch-Ambroise Bébian initiated the signed language reading movement. The logic was that if Natural Sign is deaf children's language, reading must then be taught in that language (see Grushkin, 2017 for a similar argument for ASL and deaf children). Bébian found himself involved in the creation of a writing system called Mimography (Lane, 1984a). The term was apparently chosen to reflect Natural Sign's 'mimetic' characterization involving hand movements. Bébian published work on Mimography in 1817 and 1820 (Lane, 1984b; alternatively 1825 as reported in Rée, 1999). Bébian can be described as belonging to a new generation of educators that were ready to pursue the concept of signed language reading. While the Paris school for the deaf was established in the 1760s, several decades passed before Bébian came into the picture and the signed language movement began.

In all of the ideas and actions that followed, Bébian did not consider how deaf children could best learn and master written French. There is no report in the literature about French educators recognizing the need for an intermediary system, for example. Although deaf children might learn to read in Natural Sign, they would still need to move towards learning and mastering written French. The idea of a conventional writing system for Natural Sign is feasible, but then deaf children would learn to read in their own language only. They could not repeat the reading process with French due to its status as a spoken language. For French educators, signed language literacy was new at the time. They wanted to focus on the basic idea that deaf children have the opportunity to read in Natural Sign. Any consideration of instructional design for cross-linguistic reading was lacking at the time.

In the United States, any form of contemporaneous signed language reading was curiously absent. There are a few reasons for this. Bébian's publications with Mimography took place after the deaf Frenchman, Laurent Clerc emigrated to the United States to work with the American collaborator, Thomas Hopkins Gallaudet to found the first permanent school for the deaf in Hartford, Connecticut in 1817. It can be said that American deaf education continued the direction that had taken place in France prior to Bébian's work (e.g., by favoring signing as a medium for instruction with deaf children). Moreover, one unfortunate situation for Bébian in France hampered the transfer of ideas from that country to the United States. Bébian was distraught over how the French school for the deaf was run, and his protests led to his dismissal (Lane, 1984b). The loss of Bébian's leadership was profound as signed language reading ceased to be a force.

The divisions among educators that began to emerge in France and elsewhere in the world did not help with the consideration and development of signed language reading. Natural Sign and signing were losing their favored position. The field of deaf education became polarized with oralism vs. manualism as reported in the literature. Educators who advocated oralism favored the use of spoken language with deaf children in the classroom and were in opposition to manualism (which favored the use of signed language; Moores, 1996). This led to the idea that Bébian's focus on reading in Natural Sign may have unintentionally contributed to the rise of oralism. It appears educators were frustrated with the lack of attention on how deaf children could become literate in French. Bébian was fully aware of bilingualism taking place in his school (with Natural Sign and French), but he did not pursue pedagogy for deaf children becoming literate in French as they did in Natural Sign. Oralism offered these educators a sense of direction by adopting what is normally pursued with hearing children. Deaf children would have to learn to speak and hopefully reading would follow, regardless of how counterintuitive that may be.

Bébian's unique accomplishment with Mimography merits some discussion. Rée (1999) provided information about this writing system. Since Bébian was a fluent signer (in addition to the fact that he could hear), he was intuitively aware of the word structure for Natural Sign. As part of helping create Mimography, the French educator "decompose[d] [signs] into combination of elementary gestures, just as spoken words are analy[z]ed, in alphabetic writing, as sequences of elementary sounds" (p. 298). Signs or signed words organized in terms of the handshape and movement parameters were considered analogous to vowels and consonants of the alphabet. A total of 150 graphemes were created to help write signs by the thousands.

The mention of how the written sequences of elementary gestures for Mimography parallel those of elementary sounds with an alphabetic system representing a spoken language demands attention. The choice of the term 'gesture' appears unusual. By definition, gestures are part of gesticulation that speakers frequently use in addition to speaking. Pointing to something or depicting a shape of something through the use of the hands is not the same as what Bébian attempted with Mimography. Mimography used more refined components of signs in the form of handshapes and movements, for example. Sound might have been a better term (vs. gesture) as it accounts for the abstract components that make up a word either in the signed or spoken form.

It is interesting to note that contemporary Deaf culture experts, Carol Padden and Tom Humphries devoted a chapter in their seminal 1988 book, *Deaf in America: Voices from a Culture,* to the concept of sound concerning deaf people. Silence is hearing people's perception that mischaracterizes deaf people's lives. It was described as "clumsy and inadequate as a way of explaining what [d]eaf people know and do" (p. 109). Deaf people "are far from silent but very loudly click, buzz, swish, pop, roar, and whir" (p. 109). Padden and Humphries went on to explain that poetry in signed language "shows how movement, as well as sound, can express notions like harmony, dissonance, resonance" (p. 108).

Several decades have passed since Padden and Humphries' book publication, and an updated use of sound for the visual modality is necessary for this paper. Even with the enlightened association of ASL with human language, deafness seems to define reading more than it should. For example, a group of deaf education experts have claimed that sounds, phonics, phonemic awareness, reading-aloud, and sounding out are for hearing children only and should not be part of deaf education (Simms, Andrews, & Smith, 2005). Signed language reading has not been relevant to deaf education experts (or in the field of deaf education as a whole). While experts may support ASL, they seem to have created constraints on how reading should be pursued for deaf children. The exclusion of important reading development features as strictly auditory phenomenon is an unfortunate (literal) interpretation when it should be more abstract and universally generalized. Unwarranted power is being given to spoken language as the only source for reading (also see Petitto, Langdon, Stone, Andriola, Kartheiser, & Cochran, 2016 for arguments regarding reading with deaf children based on the notion that ASL is a soundless language).

Embracing sound in the visual modality for this paper promises to help educators 'think outside the box' and become receptive to the idea of signed language reading. All languages have abstract sound elements, some are auditory and some are visual in nature. This interpretation creates a link for young deaf readers who need signed language-based phonology as a crucial element for fully experiencing the human reading process. More discussion on this will follow in connection with glossing later in this paper. Returning to Bébian, he was, by all accounts, a remarkable educator who saw something of value in signed language reading. He was bold in creating Mimography, with the assumption that deaf children are much like hearing children. While reading takes place in an entirely different language modality (i.e., signed), the underlying principles for reading remain the same.

While the concept of Mimography has merit, the system which was developed faced some deficiencies. There are conditions to consider for the creation of writing systems, especially those belonging to the alphabetic type. An ideal alphabet would have a small number of graphemes, for example (i.e., 20 to 35; Havelock, 1976). Mimography has a very large number of graphemes, which is not a good feature (S. Supalla, McKee, & Cripps, 2014). Supporting this, one deaf education expert wrote in the 1850s that Bébian's writing system "was so cumbersome as to be almost unusable; but at the same time it was not refined enough to distinguish between different signs" (Rée, 1999, p. 304). Such observation also suggested that the lack of knowledge associated with modern signed language linguistics during Bébian's time may have played a role. For example, there is strong agreement among linguists that signed words are made up of three phonological parameters, handshape, location, and movement (e.g., Brentari, 1995, 2002; Zeshan, 2002). If these three parameters were included in Mimography (and not just the handshape and the movement), there may have been a more successful writing system developed.

A Comeback for Signed Language Reading

The research climate for embracing signed language reading is ripe, for several reasons. But before proceeding, it is necessary to discuss terminology. The name, Natural Sign is no longer suitable. After Natural Sign was brought to the United States from France (through the work of Clerc and Gallaudet), it became linguistically distinct over time. Consequently, the language of deaf children living in the United States has an updated name, that is, American Sign Language. While French Sign Language continues in France (see T. Supalla & Clark, 2015 for the historical emergence of ASL as a language), any discussion of signed language reading in the United States needs to refer to ASL. Until the 1970s, ASL was written off as a human language for a perceived lack of linguistic principles, which can be seen as a block for any serious consideration associated with signed language reading. However, that has changed. ASL has won recognition as a legitimate human language owing to extensive research led by linguists in recent decades (Meier, 2002; see Sandler & Lillo-Martin, 2006 for an in-depth discussion on the linguistic structure of ASL). The common terminology in linguistics such as phonology, morphology, and syntax have been successfully extended to the signed language modality.

This points out the importance of reading terminology becoming common to signed language as well. Important reading development features such as sounds, phonics, phonemic awareness, reading-aloud, and sounding out need to be fully understood in terms of deaf readers in order to help legitimize signed language reading. Likewise, research on language acquisition has produced insights that have confirmed the legitimacy of ASL. Humans are endowed with the ability to acquire and master language. They are active learners when languages are real and meaningful to them and the language learning experience is effortless and without any formal instruction. Deaf children are no exception to that rule. They must have control over the linguistic input, a condition which is achieved with a signed language, where hearing capacity is not a prerequisite (see Newport & Meier, 1985 for an overview on ASL acquisition studies; also Schick, 2011). Denying deaf children access to ASL has been suggested by scholars to be a practice that is harmful and that must be stopped (e.g., Humphries, Kushalnagar, Mathur, Napoli, Padden, & Rathmann, 2012; see S. Supalla & Cripps, 2008 for further discussion of the linguistic accessibility concept).

For the record, many researchers and scholars outside the field of deaf education have freely discussed the idea of a writing system for ASL (e.g., Hopkins, 2008; Miller, 2001; Reagan, 2006; Turner, 2009; van der Hulst & Channon, 2010). Written language is considered a valuable asset for many spoken languages around the world. The same benefits apply to ASL (Grushkin, 2017), but the education establishment needs to rally around teaching literacy skills to deaf children based on the concept of linguistic accessibility (i.e., deaf children must learn to read in ASL, not English). Further, among the lessons learned from history is that deaf children should not be confined to learning to read in ASL only. The solution can be found in glossing, which has a specific way of handling written ASL in a way which helps deaf children decode and pursue English literacy.

Perhaps the most powerful pressure for pursuing signed language reading lies in society's push towards best reading instruction practices for all children. Deaf children are seen as part of a larger agenda for literacy. The public opinion favoring accountability is strong, which includes the understanding that deaf children cannot continue to struggle in becoming fluent readers (e.g., Marschark, Lang, & Albertini, 2002; Traxler, 2000). Of relevance for this paper is how some scholars have pointed to the importance of aligning the curriculum, instruction, and assessment to help children learn to read more successfully (Elliott, Braden, & White, 2001; Roach, Neibling, & Kurz, 2008). These scholars may not have any direct affiliation with deaf education, but the deep underlying problem with American education appears to have been identified. That is, curriculum, instruction, and assessment have been rigidly maintained, regardless of what the children need. Any pursuit of signed language reading with deaf children will require a significant amount of alignment to curriculum, instruction, and assessment.

The path for pursuing signed language reading, especially in the form of an intermediary system linking ASL and English literacy, is wide open according to Wauters and de Klerk (2014):

> ...[deaf] students in bilingual education settings, learning to read coincides with learning the language that they are reading in, and maybe even with learning their first language, sign language (Hermans, Knoors, Ormel, & Verhoeven, 2008; Hoffmeister, 2000; Markshark & Harris, 1996). Learning to read in a second language is a challenge in itself, but even more so when the learner has little access to the spoken form of that second language that is the basis of the writing system he must learn to tackle. We do not know how deaf readers make the connection between the languages they encounter (Easterbrooks & Beal-Alvarez, 2013). (p. 243)

This admission that deaf education experts made in regard to the lack of pedagogical reading knowledge for deaf children is noteworthy (see also Hoffmeister & Caldwell-Harris, 2014 for a similar admission for the lack of a method). However, they overlooked the fact that a charter school in Arizona had already put together what is known as the glossing approach to reading instruction. While traditional settings for deaf education include either schools for the deaf or programs in regular public schools that serve deaf children, it is easy to understand how charter schools may not be seen as credible or 'part of the system'.

Yet charter schools were expected to explore and test new ideas (Finn, Jr., Manno, & Vanourek, 2000). Signed language reading was identified as an innovation worthy of exploration at the Arizona charter school. The Arizona Board of Charter Schools reviewed the application and approved it leading to the school's founding in 1996. For financial reasons, the charter school could not continue after six years of operation. This did not stop a substantial amount of research and scholarly work from being published.

At the time of the Arizona charter school's founding, both educators and researchers at the charter school had full knowledge of ASL writing systems in existence (e.g., SignFont, see Newkirk, 1987; SignWriting, see Sutton, 1999). However, glossing was adopted at the school, which ultimately set it on a different course. It is important to understand that glossing is not new nor is it confined to the education of deaf children. To demonstrate the long history associated with glossing, Roby (1999) wrote:

> ...early glosses, interlinear or marginal scribblings, were learner-generated. Medieval students struggling with a foreign text (usually Latin) produced them as they worked along. Glosses as teaching aids came later, followed by their eventual codification into word lists (glossaries) and then dictionaries. (p. 94)

The reading challenge that medieval students faced with Latin is comparable to deaf children with English literacy. Latin was a 'dead language', meaning it was no longer spoken (which was historically true after the fall of the Roman Empire). The medieval students did not have an opportunity to hear Latin and use that knowledge for reading development purposes. These students found themselves scribbling down information on how to best read Latin. It is such interlinear translation that allowed the medieval students to write about how the structure and grammar of Latin compared to the language that they knew. It is easy to imagine how other students could read the gloss passages to help learn to read Latin. More discussion on this for how glossing applies to deaf children's learning will follow in the next section.

In addition, the modern use of glossaries and dictionaries which help students who can hear and know English points to the universal benefits associated with glossing. Native English speaking students who are already literate often encounter unknown 'big words' in print. They are provided with the opportunity to look up definitions and understand the individual words' meanings in a dictionary. Second language learners of English have a similar option with glossing as well. The three well-known types of glossing for this group of students are: 1) synonyms, 2) encyclopedic comments, and 3) grammatical notes (Roby, 1999). The description of glossing as "a common and acceptable aid for many foreign language textbooks" (Lomicka, 1998, p. 41) should be noted. From what has been discussed for glossing thus far, it appears that the primary function of glossing is to make text clear. Deaf children are entitled to glossing as English text is unclear and unreadable.

Making English Readable for Deaf Children

As expected for curriculum, instruction, and assessment alignment, the glossing approach adopted at the Arizona charter school had an impact on what reading materials looked like, how a teacher taught reading skills, and how deaf children's reading skills were assessed. The educators and researchers were sensitive to the fact that deaf children enrolled at the charter school were young and had not yet learned to read (e.g., kindergartners). Recall that medieval students would read gloss passages attached to Latin text. The medieval students were older and accomplished readers. They read in their own language to learn about Latin. No truly intermediary system is in use here. This is where the idea of doing more by glossing the English text itself emerged at the charter school. The English text was manipulated to the point that it resembled ASL's morpho-syntactic structure. To distinguish an ASL text from that of a regular text, the printed English words or roots are fully capitalized. The ordering of words in a given sentence may be changed (as ASL has a flexible word order as compared to English). A set of conventions were created to help fully represent ASL's grammatical structure by using an underline or a symbol attached to the beginning or end of a basic English word or root, for example.

True to the objective of glossing, the English text is made clear to deaf children through the necessary manipulation. The children at the charter school could read the text word by word when it was consistent with ASL morphologically and syntactically. It is important to note that text manipulation has been recognized as a way of improving reading performance for all children. Ralabate (2011) explained that text manipulation is critical for improving the reading outcomes of students with disabilities. For whatever reading difficulties there may be, the text itself can be problematic and manipulation can make all the difference.

Hundreds of gloss books were created at the charter school, derived from children's literature and basal readers. It is now necessary to explain what gloss text looks like exactly. The basis for creating gloss text is interlinear translation. The English sentence example below showing before and after manipulation will help clarify the technique:

Before Manipulation: The dog is chasing the cat.

After Manipulation: DOG NOW CHASE>IX=3 CAT

S. Supalla and Cripps (2011) produced the sentence examples above and provided a detailed description of how glossing took place with the original English sentence as follows:

> [The gloss sentence] depicts four English words all capitalized to represent the four signs produced as an equivalent of the English sentence composed of the six words... [s]tructurally, no definite article is used in the ASL gloss sentence, which is correct for the signed language. The ASL gloss sentence also indicates a rough equivalence of the present progressive tense in English, with the insertion of NOW as a separate word (or "time sign") before the verb. In addition, the ASL verb CHASE undergoes a third person object agreement inflection (i.e., the movement of the verb is [modified] to agree with the location of the cat in the

signing space) with the attachment of the gloss convention >IX=3 to the verb representing inflection in the sentence. (p. 4)

What has been discussed so far relates to the sentence level. The educators and researchers at the charter school took into consideration the fact that the gloss text includes the use of English words. A hearing child would sound out or decode an unfamiliar word in print to help with his or her reading comprehension. Clearly, deaf children cannot do this task, but those at the charter school were provided with a way to identify English words in the gloss text. This is where a supporting component of the glossing approach comes in, called The Resource Book (RB). The RB works like a bilingual dictionary with thousands of English words paired with the ASL equivalents written in what is called the ASL-phabet.

With the gloss sentence, DOG NOW CHASE>IX=3 CAT, a young deaf child reading this sentence might be able to identify all words except for CAT. The child could then use the RB to locate the word and then read the ASL equivalent next to it. The written sign for CAT is: ᖷ ᴐ ꙅ ᴎ. S. Supalla and Cripps explained the details associated with this written sign as follows:

> In the ASL equivalent for CAT, the grapheme in the furthest left slot refers to the handshape seen in Figure [1] below, the next grapheme refers to the location of where the sign is produced (i.e., on the cheek), and the last graphemes refer to the movements made (i.e., ꙅ = straight path and ᴎ = repeated). (p. 7)

Figure 1: The sign for CAT

Here the deaf child could sound out the sign and learn the meaning of the English word. The child can then read and comprehend the gloss sentence (i.e., the dog is chasing a cat, not a rabbit, for example) and move on to reading other sentences. As demonstrated here, the RB makes a clear connection between English words and their ASL equivalents.

In comparison to what was discussed for Mimography, it becomes clear that the ASL-phabet is designed for the word level only, not sentences or text (as done with the French system). Moreover, the ASL-phabet accounts for three phonological parameters of handshape, location, and movement (which can be seen as an improvement). The number of graphemes for the ASL-phabet, this time, falls in line with what was discussed above for an ideal alphabet. The ASL-phabet has 32 graphemes in use (i.e., 20 graphemes for the handshape parameter, 5 for the location parameter, and 5 for the movement parameter). Aggressive grouping of handshapes within single graphemes played a key role, which helped dramatically reduce the number of graphemes in comparison to Mimography. The same holds true for the location and movement parameters (see S. Supalla et al., 2014 for further discussion on the ASL-phabet as a system).

Teachers at the Arizona charter school found themselves teaching phonics in ASL owing to some phonological ambiguity in how signs are written based on the ASL-phabet. For example, the handshape grapheme for CAT, ᐯo represents two handshapes, not one. As shown in Figure 2, these two handshapes are closely related sounds with a slight difference in how the hand is shaped. Deaf children at the school were taught about sound representation in the handshape parameter. The same holds true for the location parameter. While the location grapheme for CAT is ᗝ (as the sign is produced on the cheek), other signs produced on the mouth or on the chin will use the same location grapheme. The grapheme ᗝ represents a more general location area of the cheek, mouth, and chin. Similar types of phonics lessons were taught on movement for the ASL-phabet as well. Since deaf children were expected to use the RB on a regular basis, they had to understand how the ASL-phabet worked and teaching phonics was critical for their success.

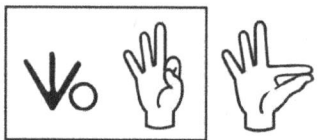

Figure 2: Two handshapes (one with rounded and one with pinched fingers) grouped for the representation of a single grapheme for the ASL-phabet

Some of the overall positive impacts of the glossing approach for reading instruction were discussed in S. Supalla, Cripps, and Byrne (2017) as follows:

Since [deaf] children can sign word for word [via gloss text], it is easy for the teacher to see if they are reading with accuracy, for example. The teacher can also monitor whether these children use [the RB] any time they encounter unfamiliar English words in print. This allows the teacher to see how the children fare with reading the ASL equivalents written in the ASL-phabet. The teacher's guidance on reading written signs will strengthen the deaf child's decoding skills. The same holds true for modeling deaf children on how to best read a gloss text with a wide range of conventions in use. One way or another, these children's reading comprehension will be boosted. Fluency will ultimately develop with practice opportunities provided along with the teacher's coaching efforts. (p. 546)

Thanks to the liberal application of key concepts for reading processes, educators and researchers at the charter school were able to foster natural skills in learning to read. While skill in making the English-based letter and sound relationships was not part of the reading instruction design at the school, deaf children were provided an opportunity to do this in an alternative fashion. They were encouraged to study ASL phonology in terms of handshapes, locations, and movements and connect them with the ASL-phabet graphemes or ASL letters. The skills associated with the ASL-phabet were treated as comparable to how the alphabetic principle is taught to students who can hear with English (S. Supalla & Blackburn, 2003).

The reading instruction curriculum, materials and teaching at the charter school included opportunities for deaf children to develop phonemic awareness in ASL (as part of their preparation for learning to read words in ASL). Kindergartners were exposed to ASL nursery rhymes as produced by accomplished signers on videotapes readily available on the market. *The ASL Parent-child Mother Goose Program: American Sign Language Rhymes, Rhythms and Stories for Parents and their Children* produced by the Ontario Cultural Society of the Deaf (2004) serves as a good example. One of the songs was rhymed throughout the production via one particular handshape. Deaf children exposed to the handshape-based rhyme were expected to develop awareness about that particular handshape.

Turning to how deaf children at the charter school experienced transition from ASL to English literacy, it is necessary to remember they were reading gloss books and using the RB on a regular basis to access meanings of the individual English words. This is precisely the way that deaf children developed a strong English vocabulary base. The English books were more readable to these children as the words were the same as found in the gloss books (e.g., cat vs. CAT, dog vs. DOG, and chase vs. CHASE). The benefits associated with the shared spelling and orthography of the gloss and regular texts form the basis for the initial transition from ASL to English literacy (S. Supalla & Cripps, 2011).

A complete transition to English literacy is realized when deaf children participate in another supporting component called Comparative Analysis. Children initially read a gloss book (and use the RB whenever necessary) and participate in different activities around that book. The teacher then introduces the children to the gloss and regular versions for observation and analysis (e.g., the gloss version: DOG NOW CHASE>IX=3 CAT with the English version: The dog is chasing the cat). With the help of the transparency between the gloss and regular texts, deaf children can study what is structurally similar and different between ASL and English and focus on learning the grammatical features that are specific to English.

The learning of English for deaf children at the charter school was repeated with one book after another, along with increasing text complexity over time. Teachers at this school appreciated the fact that the less complex texts for younger readers coincided with rudimentary English structures to learn. The older readers could review what they learned and study the new and more complex structures over time. This resulted in the scaffolding of the English language skills that deaf children needed to learn and master over time (S. Supalla & Cripps, 2011).

By the fourth grade, deaf children at the charter school were expected to read to learn (rather than learn to read). They needed to demonstrate their reading performance through assessment. One example of information gathered from deaf children is how well they read aloud a gloss text with their performance measured through what is known as running records (Clay, 2000). Deaf children were asked to read the English text silently, and answer a set of comprehension questions. With a good or satisfactory level of performance with ASL and English, the glossing approach for reading instruction would cease. At that point, deaf children would be reading in English and continue using ASL for communicative purposes in the classroom (see S. Supalla & Blackburn, 2003 for the further discussion on the phasing out of the glossing approach).

Some Indications of Signed Language Reading

To begin with, adequate signed language reading research has never been presented on Mimography. Bébian did report on deaf children's performance with reading in French Sign Language when he described the writing system's success as questionable. Rée (1999) wrote that "...Bébian's own claim that the 150 characters of [M]imography could be mastered by a deaf signer within 'eight or ten days' had a quality of crazed desperation..." (p. 301). The earlier discussion of the internal problems with the French Sign Language writing system suggests that the French effort with signed language reading should not be pursued. The fact that multiple research publications have been produced in regard to signed language reading at the American charter school is most welcoming. This includes valuable data on how well deaf children perform in reading gloss text, as it is unconventional and has no precedence in the general literature on glossing. A variety of reading behaviors to follow that deaf children have demonstrated are promising.

The first known publication on signed language reading with deaf children in the United States is the S. Supalla, Wix, and McKee paper (2001). The data is descriptive in nature. Deaf kindergarteners at the charter school learning to read their name signs written in the ASL-phabet were subject to videotaping for later analysis. The description of the particular classroom activity led by the teacher is:

> The teacher showed one card at a time and asked the class who the written name referred to. The students recognized their names by looking at the first two graphemes (i.e., handshape and location information). They signed their names to indicate that they recognized the written names. The students were clearly engaged in the activity. (p. 9)

The authors of the paper went on to write:

> ...deaf students 'read' words with only partial information (i.e., handshape-location/symbol relationships) and the context of a name-reading exercise. This is comparable to the kinds of early success that hearing kindergartners get when first identifying consonant sound/symbol relationships in the context of words they are learning. At the [Arizona charter school], such activities show the beginning development of metalinguistic awareness for ASL signs. [Teachers] start children on the handshape and location graphemes in kindergarten and first grade. Movement graphemes are mastered first through third grade levels. (pp. 9-10)

The detailed nature of how skills were taught at the charter school supported the Arizona Academic Standards' reading component, which dictates that kindergartners begin identifying words in print through consonants (whereas vowels are more difficult to learn and master). It is interesting to note that the teachers at the charter school were not sure how to teach deaf children in reading signs at first. The children's learning patterns ultimately shaped the instruction design with the ASL-phabet. The handshape-location/symbol relationships were easier to learn as compared to the movement/symbol relationships, thus the former was seen as involving consonants and the latter vowels. There is support for such a signed word structure in the ASL linguistics community. Diane Brentari, a well-known and highly reputable linguist presented an argument in a 2002 paper about the existence of consonants and vowels in ASL words. The combined handshape and location information of a given sign falls under the consonant category while the movement information is considered the vowel category.

Recall that, with Mimography, Bébian treated the handshape information of French signs as the consonant equivalent and the movement as the vowel equivalent. While the distinction between consonants and vowels that contemporary scholars and researchers are pursuing is more refined (by accounting for the combined handshape and location information, not just the handshape information), the basic distinction between the handshape parameter and that of movement is still true for both systems, the ASL-phabet and Mimography. At the time when the ASL-phabet was developed at the Arizona charter school, educators and researchers were not aware of these details associated with Mimography. The consonants and vowels in signed words identified uniformly among the different educators and researchers during contemporary times stretching back to the early nineteenth century suggests that the credibility of such understanding for signed word structure is strong.

S. Supalla et al. (2014) provided additional insights on signed language reading at the word level. The data, this time, involves an older (9 years old) deaf child. This child was a student at the Arizona charter school and participated in a tutorial during one summer. The child was required to look at a set of four flashcards held by the tutor. On each flashcard was the written sign for 'correct', 'on', 'day' and 'long'. The written signs were unfamiliar to the child. The child was asked to read each word and tell what it was. The tutor explained to the child that he would only tell whether the response was correct or incorrect. If not correct, the child was encouraged to try to read the word again to hopefully come up with the correct sign. The choice for what sign to come up with was wide open. The task was quite challenging, but thought to be appropriate for the older child.

According to the data, this child was successful with the written sign 'long'. She read the word and responded with the correct sign. In the process of decoding what the ASL word was, the child moved her hands 'in the air' trying to come up with the correct sign. One could tell that the child took into consideration the consonant and vowel information in print. With the three other written signs, the child was less successful. She responded with incorrect signs before signing the correct word. In the deaf child's 'failed' responses, the signs were all close to the target sign phonologically. The child was trying her best to come up with the correct sign based on what she read on the card.

While the deaf child discussed thus far was not fluent with reading written signs, she did read all of the words written on the cards when given another chance:

> The flashcard activity included one more stop, which was reviewing the four words with the child. When the tutor mixed the order of the four words and showed them to the child again, she responded correctly to all words. Regardless of the fact that the child had most trouble with ['correct']. She read it perfectly during the review of the four words. (p. 15)

The assessment method in the paper by Cripps and S. Supalla (2004) is somewhat different. This time, a well-known vocabulary test was given to deaf children participating in the study. The word items in the Peabody Picture Vocabulary Test-Revised (Dunn & Dunn, 1981; Jongsma, 1982; Kipps & Hanson, 1983) were converted from spoken to print to allow deaf children to see the words (instead of hearing them). The two deaf children participating in the study were instructed to go through a list of English words and respond to each word by pointing to the correct picture out of four in a booklet. The children were provided with the Resource Book or RB to help with their English word identification. They were instructed to use the RB at all times regardless of whether they knew the English word or not.

It is important to keep in mind that the two deaf children who participated in the study differed in age and schooling experience. The first child was Lucy (pseudonym) who was 6:11 years old, and the second child was Barb (again a pseudonym) who was 9:11 years old. Lucy enrolled at the Arizona charter school at the age of 4 and had been taught at this school for three years. Barb was with the charter school for two years. Prior to transferring to the charter school, she was in a traditional school for the deaf (where the glossing approach of reading instruction was not implemented).

According to Cripps and S. Supalla, Lucy "began the test at the 10th vocabulary item, *reading*...[s]he reached the ceiling at the 49th vocabulary item, *coin*" (p. 105). What is important for this paper is that the majority of English words were identified successfully: "Lucy looked up a total of 38 words using [the RB]. She produced 30 correct answers out of the 38 vocabulary items (or 72%). She could not identify 8 English words after reading the ASL equivalents in [the RB]" (p. 105).

Barb began the test at the 30th vocabulary item, *whale*. She reached the ceiling at the 90th vocabulary item, *triplet*. As with Lucy, Barb identified a majority of the English words in the test successfully. This child did not use the RB consistently, however. The following discussion of her performance will clarify the differences:

> Barb looked up a total of 51 words using [the RB] out of 59 vocabulary items (or 86%). With the 51 words, she produced 32 correct answers (or 62%). She could not identify 19 English words after reading the ASL equivalent[s] in [the RB]. (p. 105)

Barb's level of English word identification performance is lower in comparison to Lucy's (62% vs. 72%). Given that Barb is older, she should have performed better than Lucy. The fact that Barb transferred to the charter school and had a shorter time of exposure to its aligned curriculum and instruction appears to be a factor.

Cripps and S. Supalla's study includes the finding that both Barb and Lucy outperformed what was normed for deaf children. With the deaf normative study done by Bunch and Forde (1987), the Peabody Vocabulary Test-Revised was subject to the same modification (i.e., the target words converted from spoken to print), without the RB in use. In comparison to the normed scores for the different ages of deaf children, Barb and Lucy, who had access to the RB, did far better in the identification of English words. This can be attributed to their making associations with ASL.

In S. Supalla et al. (2017), the focus is on reading at the sentence level. One 9-year-old child participated in the study, and she read aloud a gloss passage (in ASL), which was reproduced in the paper. Specifically, running records were utilized with the child reading the gloss passage matching her age. A word count formula was created for ASL to help with effective computation (being sensitive not just to counting signs in a given sentence, but for other features such as facial syntactic markers and classifier constructions). The child's oral reading performance was found to be at the instructional level. The age-appropriate gloss text was not too difficult or too easy. The child was capable of reading, but not yet an independent or fluent reader. She read the gloss passage with accuracy for the most part. Some predictable reading behaviors such as skipping a word and making a self-correction occurred, but they were not enough to hamper the reading process. The child used the RB once for an unfamiliar word that she encountered, which was IN-A-HURRY. The English word identification was successful, and the child signed the word and continued reading the rest of the gloss passage.

Closing Remarks

The research reports for deaf children using the glossing approach for reading instruction at the word and sentence levels have ramifications for the field of deaf education. The various reading behaviors point to the reality of signed language reading. The skills are measurable or observable, at least preliminarily. The key concepts associated with sounds, phonics, phonemic awareness, reading-aloud, and sounding out are internal to signed language reading. It is important to keep in mind that the research reports discussed in this paper cover the glossing approach to reading instruction partially. What has yet to be discussed (based on the data) is how deaf children experience a full transition to English literacy through the perusal of comparative analysis and the teaching of English language lessons on regular basis. This component is integral to the glossing approach as much as the gloss books and the RB. A future paper will need to include the comparative analysis lessons as taught in the classroom and demonstrate how deaf children participate and learn about English.

In addition, any coverage on how deaf children make progress with signed language-based reading skills over time is lacking. Publishing a doctoral dissertation work on this topic (Cripps, 2008) will be an important step, as the results can be positive and insightful. For now, while the number of deaf students whose data is included in this paper is small, it is still appropriate for understanding the feasibility of signed language reading. As a whole, the signed language reading research is in its infancy, yet primed for expansion.

The importance of signed language reading cannot be further emphasized. Easterbrooks (2010) explained that "the evidence base in deaf education tends to be woefully lacking" (p. 111) is a serious matter. Because reading has been equated with spoken language, teachers of the deaf are stymied in what they can do about reading instruction. This environment is not conducive to creating or gathering evidence for best practices when reading is tied to hearing ability. With this paper, deaf education experts can now consider the glossing approach for teaching reading to deaf children, especially with its cross-linguistic features. The notion of deaf children using ASL to decode English (as part of becoming literate in a language they do not hear) is attractive in its own right. This option exceeds what reading theories offer (as they focus on how children become literate in one language at a time). Shaping the education of deaf children based on what hearing children experience with reading is inappropriate and restrictive. Reading theories need to account for all children, including those who are deaf and have a unique way of learning and mastering English literacy.

In retrospect, the basic idea of signed language reading first attempted in nineteenth century France where deaf children learned to read in French Sign Language is something that all teachers of the deaf should know and appreciate. The resurgence of signed language reading as reported for a charter school in the United States centers on a more complex framework connecting ASL to English literacy. This is where text manipulation comes into the picture and becomes the key component of signed language reading. The curriculum, instruction, and assessment alignment is also found to be necessary to ensure that deaf children experience a meaningful reading methodology. It is hoped that in the near future, glossing as a reading methodology and its different tools and procedures including gloss books, the RB, and comparative analysis lessons can prove themselves as a staple in the education of deaf children. No longer would these children be plagued by reading difficulties, but perhaps their exposure to signed language-based teachings can clear a path towards English literacy.

References

Adams, M. J. (1990). *Beginning to read: Thinking and learning about print.* Cambridge, MA: MIT Press.

Brentari, D. (1995). Sign language phonology: ASL. In J. Goldsmith (Ed.), *A handbook of phonological theory* (pp. 615-639). New York, NY: Basil Blackwell.

Brentari, D. (2002). Modality differences in sign language phonology and morphophonemics. In R. P. Meier, K. Cormier, & D. Quinto-Pozos (Eds.), *Modality and structure in signed and spoken languages* (pp. 35-64). Cambridge, UK: Cambridge University Press.

Bunch, G. O., & Forde, J. (1987). Pilot standardization of the Peabody Picture Vocabulary Test-Revised on hearing impaired subjects. *A.C.E.H.I. Journal, 12*(3), 165-170.

Clay, M. M. (2000). *Running records for classroom teachers.* Portsmouth, NH: Heinemann.

Cripps, J. H. (2008). *A case study on reading processes of signing deaf children* (Unpublished doctoral dissertation). University of Arizona, Tucson, AZ.

Cripps, J. H., & Supalla, S. J. (2004). Modifications to the Peabody Picture Vocabulary Test for use with deaf students. *Arizona Working Papers in Second Language Acquisition and Teaching, 11*, 93-113. Tucson, AZ: University of Arizona.

Dunn, L. M., & Dunn, L. M. (1981). *Peabody Picture Vocabulary Test-Revised manual for Forms L and M.* Circle Pines, MN: American Guidance Service, Inc.

Easterbrooks, S. R. (2010). Evidence-based curricula and practices that support development of reading skills. In M. Marschark & P. E. Spencer (Eds.), *The Oxford handbook of deaf studies, language, and education* (Vol. 2, pp. 111-126). New York, NY: The Oxford University Press.

Easterbrooks, S. R., & Beal-Alvarez, J. (2013). *Literacy instruction for students who are deaf and hard of hearing.* Oxford, UK: Oxford University Press.

Elliott, S. N., Braden, J. P., & White, J. L. (2001). *Assessing one and all: Educational accountability for students with disabilities.* Arlington, VA: Council Exceptional Children.

Finn, C. E., Jr., Manno, B. V., & Vanourek, G. (2000). *Charter schools in action: Renewing public education.* Princeton, NJ: Princeton University Press.

Goldin-Meadow, S., & Mayberry, R. I. (2001). How do profoundly deaf children learn to read? *Learning Disabilities Research & Practice, 16*(4), 222-229.

Grabe, W. (2009). *Reading in a second language: Moving from theory to practice.* Cambridge, UK: Cambridge University Press.

Grushkin, D. A. (2017). Writing signed languages: What for? What form? *American Annals of the Deaf, 161*(5), 509-527.

Havelock, E. (1976). Origins of Western literacy. *The Ontario Institute for Studies in Education Monograph Series, 14.*

Hermans, D., Knoors, H., Ormel, E., & Verhoeven, L. (2008). The relationship between the reading and signing skills of deaf children in bilingual education programs. *Journal of Deaf Studies and Deaf Education, 13*(4), 518-530.

Hoffmeister, R. J. (2000). A piece of puzzle: ASL and reading comprehension in deaf children. In C. Chamberlain, J. P. Morford, & R. I. Mayberry (Eds.), *Language acquisition by eye* (pp. 143-163). Mahwah, NJ: Lawrence Erlbaum.

Hoffmeister, R. J., & Caldwell-Harris, C. L. (2014). Acquiring English as a second language via print: The task for deaf children. *Cognition, 132*(2), 229-242.

Hoover, W. A., & Gough, P. G. (1990). The simple view of reading. *Reading and Writing: An Interdisciplinary Journal, 2*(2), 127-160.

Hopkins, J. (2008). Choosing how to write sign language: A sociolinguistic perspective. *International Journal of the Sociology of Language, 192,* 75-89.

Humphries, T., Kushalnagar, P., Mathur, G., Napoli, D. J., Padden, C., Rathmann, C., & Smith, S. R. (2012). Language acquisition for deaf children: Reducing the harms of zero tolerance to the use of alternative approaches. *Harm Reduction Journal, 9*(16).

Jongsma, E. A. (1982). Test review: Peabody Picture Vocabulary Test-Revised (PPVT-R). *Journal of Reading, 25*(4), 360-364.

Kipps, D., & Hanson, D. (1983). Test review: The revised PPVT. *School Psychology Review, 12*(1), 112-113.

Koda, K. (2005). *Insights into second language reading: A cross-linguistic approach.* Cambridge, UK: Cambridge University Press.

Lane, H. (Ed.). (1984a). *The deaf experience: Classics in language and education* (F. Phillips, Trans.). Cambridge, MA: Harvard University Press.

Lane, H. (1984b). *When the mind hears: A history of the deaf.* New York, NY: First Vintage Books.

Lane, H., Hoffmeister, R., & Bahan, B. (1996). *A journey into the deaf-world.* San Diego, CA: DawnSignPress.

Lomicka, L. L. (1998). "To gloss or not to gloss": An investigation of reading comprehension online. *Language Learning & Technology, 1*(2), 41-50.

Markshark, M., & Harris, M. (1996). Success and failure in learning to read: The special (?) case of deaf children. In C. Cornoldi & J. Oakhill (Eds.), *Reading comprehension difficulties: Processes and intervention* (pp. 279-300). Hillside, NJ: Lawrence Erlbaum.

Marschark, M., Lang, H. G., & Albertini, J. A. (2002). *Educating deaf students: From research to practice.* Oxford, UK: Oxford University Press.

Mayer, C., & Wells, G. (1996). Can the linguistic interdependence theory support a bilingual-bicultural model of literacy education for deaf students? *Journal of Deaf Studies and Deaf Education, 1*(2), 93-107.

Meier, R. P. (2002). Why different, why the same? Explaining the effects and non-effects of modality upon linguistic structure in sign and speech. In R. P. Meier, K. Cormier, & D. Quinto-Pozos (Eds.), *Modality and structure in signed and spoken languages* (pp. 1-26). Cambridge, UK: Cambridge University Press.

Miller, C. (2001). Some reflections on the need for a common sign notation. *Sign Language & Linguistics, 4*(1/2), 11-28.

Moores, D. F. (1996). *Educating the deaf: Psychology, principles, and practices* (4th ed.). Boston, MA: Houghton Mifflin.

Newkirk, D. (1987). *Architect: Final version SignFont handbook.* San Diego, CA: Salk Institute and Emerson and Stern Associates.

Newport, E. L., & Meier, R. (1985). The acquisition of American Sign Language. In D. I. Slobin (Ed.), *The crosslinguistic study of language acquisition: The data* (Vol. 1). Hillside, NJ: Lawrence Erlbaum.

Ontario Cultural Society of the Deaf. (2004). *The ASL parent-child mother goose program: American Sign Language rhymes, rhythms and stories for parents and their children* [DVD]. Ontario Cultural Society of the Deaf Project.

Padden, C., & Humphries, T. (1988). *Deaf in America: Voices from a culture.* Cambridge, MA: Harvard University Press.

Paul, P. V. (1994). Response to "Unlocking the curriculum": Principles for achieving access in deaf education. *Teaching English to Deaf and Second-Language Students, 10*(2), 18-21.

Paul, P. V., & Quigley, S. P. (1987). Using American Sign Language to teach English. In P. L. McAnally, S. Rose, & S. P. Quigley (Eds.), *Language learning practices with deaf children* (pp. 139-166). Boston, MA: College-Hill Press.

Petitto, L. A., Langdon, C., Stone, A., Andriola, D., Kartheiser, G., & Cochran, C. (2016). *Visual sign phonology: Insights into human reading and language from a natural soundless phonology.* WIREs Cognitive Science.

Ralabate, P. K. (2011). Universal design for learning: Meeting the needs of all students. *The ASHA Leader, 16*, 14-17.

Reagan, T. (2006). Language policy and sign languages. In T. Ricento (Ed.), *An introduction to language policy: Theory and method* (pp. 329-345). Oxford, UK: Blackwell.

Rée, J. (1999). *I see a voice: Deafness, language and the senses – A philosophical history.* New York, NY: Metropolitan Books.

Roach, A. T., Neibling, B. C., & Kurz, A. (2008). Evaluating the alignment among curriculum, instruction, and assessments: Implications and applications for research and practice. *Psychology in the Schools, 45*(2), 158-176.

Roby, W. B. (1999). What's in a gloss? *Language Learning & Technology, 2*(2), 94-101.

Sandler, W., & Lillo-Martin, D. (2006). *Sign language and linguistic universals.* Cambridge, UK: Cambridge University Press.

Schick, B. (2011). The development of American Sign Language and manually coded English systems. In M. Marschark & E. Spencer (Eds.), *Oxford handbook of deaf studies, language, and education* (2nd ed., pp. 229-240). Oxford, UK: Oxford University Press.

Simms, L., Andrews, J., & Smith, A. (2005). A balanced approach to literacy instruction for deaf signing students. *Balanced Reading Instruction, 12*, 39-54.

Singleton, J. L., Supalla, S. J., Litchfield, S., & Schley, S. (1998). From sign to word: Considering modality constraints in ASL/English bilingual education. *Topics in Language Disorders, 18*(4), 16-29.

Snow, C. E., Burns, M. S., & Griffin, P. (Eds.). (1998). *Preventing reading difficulties in young children.* Washington, DC: National Academy Press.

Supalla, S. J., & Blackburn, L. (2003). Learning how to read and bypassing sound. *Odyssey, 5*(1), 50-55.

Supalla, S. J., & Cripps, J. H. (2008). Linguistic accessibility and deaf children. In B. Spolsky & F. Hult (Eds.), *The handbook of educational linguistics* (pp. 174-191). Oxford, UK: Blackwell.

Supalla, S. J., & Cripps, J. H. (2011). Toward universal design in reading instruction. *Bilingual Basics, 12*(2).

Supalla, S. J., Cripps, J. H., & Byrne, A. P. J. (2017). Why American Sign Language gloss must matter. *American Annals of the Deaf, 161*(5), 540-551.

Supalla, S. J., & McKee, C. (2002). The role of manually coded English in language development of deaf children. In R. Meier, K. Cormier, & D. Quinto-Pozos (Eds.), *Modality and structure in signed and spoken languages* (pp. 143-165). Cambridge, UK: Cambridge University Press.

Supalla, S. J., McKee C., & Cripps, J. H. (2014). *An overview on the ASL-phabet*. Tucson, AZ: The Gloss Institute Press.

Supalla, S. J., Wix, T. R., & McKee, C. (2001). Print as a primary source of English for deaf learners. In J. Nicol & T. Langendoen (Eds.), *One mind, two languages: Studies in bilingual language processing* (pp. 177-190). Oxford, UK: Blackwell.

Supalla, T., & Clark, P. (2015). *Sign language archaeology: Understanding the historical roots of American Sign Language*. Washington, DC: Gallaudet University Press.

Sutton, V. (1999). SignWriting. *Sign Language & Linguistics, 2*(2), 271-282.

Traxler, C. B. (2000). The Stanford Achievement Test, 9th edition: National norming and performance standards for deaf and hard of hearing students. *Journal of Deaf Studies and Deaf Education, 5*(4), 337-348.

Turner, G. H. (2009). Sign language planning: Pragmatism, pessimism and principles. *Current Issues in Language Planning, 10*(3), 243-254.

Van Cleve, J. V., & Crouch, B. A. (1989). *A place of their own: Creating the deaf community in America*. Washington, DC: Gallaudet University Press.

van der Hulst, H., & Channon, R. (2010). Notation systems. In D. Brentari (Ed.), *Sign languages* (pp. 151-172). Cambridge, UK: Cambridge University Press.

Wauters, L., & de Klerk, A. (2014). Improving reading instruction to deaf and hard-of-hearing students. In M. Marschark, G. Tang, & H. Knoors (Eds.), *Bilingualism and bilingual deaf education* (pp. 242-271). New York, NY: Oxford University Press.

Zeshan, U. (2002). Towards a notion of "word" in sign languages. In R. M. W. Dixon & A. Y. Aikhenvald (Eds.), *Word: A cross-linguistic typology* (pp. 153-179). Cambridge, UK: Cambridge University Press.

American Sign Language Literature:
Some Considerations for Legitimacy and Quality Issues

Andrew P. J. Byrne
Framingham State University

Abstract

American Sign Language (ASL) literature is a recent phenomenon in the American and Canadian academic landscape and constitutes an important component for the field of ASL and Deaf Studies. There are a number of pressing issues that have not been addressed until now. These include: how to respond to the status of ASL as a non-written language, various definitions for ASL literature, a large number of literary works translated from English to ASL, and the confusion associated with some works being produced by the deaf community as opposed to those by individual performers. This paper represents an attempt to address these issues. The four main objectives of this paper are: (1) to validate the relationship between oral literature and ASL literature; (2) to provide a comprehensive definition for ASL literature; (3) to promote the value of originality as compared to translation; and (4) to create a taxonomy of ASL literary genres. Substantial information and some research data is presented which comes from the author's doctoral dissertation, completed in 2013. A comprehensive definition of ASL literature is expected to help maintain the legitimacy and quality of the literary language of the deaf community. The author has been involved in the creation of a collection of ASL literary works, which provides a much-needed basis for research and scholarship. The general knowledge of ASL literature through the familiarity with works listed in the collection will help create a canon of ASL literature.

Introduction

At present, American Sign Language (ASL) enjoys popularity as a language to study. The Modern Language Association reported that student enrollment in signed language coursework is growing much faster than other languages in the American higher education setting (Furman, Goldberg, & Lusin, 2010; Goldberg, Looney, & Lusin, 2015; McQuillan, 2012). The inclusion of literature in any language study is important, and ASL should not be treated as an exception to the rule. ASL literature provides students with keen insights on the people who use signed language. Deaf people in the United States and parts of Canada are the primary users of ASL. They have formed and maintain a community that shares features of ethnic communities (Lane, Pillard, & Hedberg, 2011). ASL has played a central role in how deaf people have become a linguistic and cultural minority in the context of society (Ladd, 2003; Lane, Hoffmeister, & Bahan, 1996; Padden, 1980; Padden & Humphries, 1988; Stokoe, 1980; Wilcox, 1989).

ASL can be seen as a latecomer to academia when it comes to how languages are traditionally taught (i.e., spoken and written). It was during the 1970s and 1980s that ASL started receiving recognition as an independent and full-fledged human language possessing a linguistic structure comprised of its own phonology, morphology, and syntax (Sandler & Lillo-Martin, 2006; Valli, Lucas, Mulrooney, & Villanueva, 2011). What is known as deaf culture further justifies the teaching of ASL as a foreign language in American and Canadian colleges and universities. There are several curricula for teaching ASL that are available for purchase (e.g., Humphries & Padden, 2004; Smith, Lentz, & Mikos, 2008; Zinza, 2006). The fact that ASL has no writing system has not stopped instructors from teaching the literary component of the signed language. However, a few decades have passed and it is time to pause and examine ASL literature in terms of legitimacy and quality. In-depth discussions about ASL literature will help affirm its value and improve its quality.

This paper discusses four main topics: (1) the relationship between oral literature and ASL literature; (2) a comprehensive definition of ASL literature; (3) the question of translation; and (4) the taxonomy of ASL literary genres. Substantial information and some data come from the author's doctoral dissertation, which was completed in 2013. This dissertation sought to develop a comprehensive definition of ASL literature and to organize its genres of original literary works. The methodology involved semi-structured interviews of eight deaf ASL users who are experts in the field of ASL and Deaf Studies. The experts had extensive knowledge of ASL literature as well as numerous years of experience teaching ASL language and literature courses. From an original pool of twelve experts, eight were available for interviews. They possessed a range of degrees from the bachelor's level through the doctoral level and positions ranging from K – 12 educators and administrators to post-secondary faculty and researchers. Interviews were conducted in person or via videophone. All interviews were video recorded. Experts were asked four research questions related to legitimacy and quality of ASL literature. The questions were as follows:

1) At a time when there is increasing recognition of ASL literacy, how should ASL literature be defined?
2) What are the features that characterize ASL literature?
3) What would constitute such a literature (e.g., genres)? To what extent is there a comprehensive taxonomy of genres captured in VHS and DVD publications?
4) What are examples of ASL literary works included in this taxonomy?

After collecting and transcribing data from the interviews, a cross-sectional analysis of the interviews was performed using a constant comparison method. The responses were analyzed and placed into categories for comparison. The process of categorizing was done by reading the transcribed text of the interviews, circling common responses, and developing categories for the responses. After completing the categorization process, the common categories were grouped around common responses for each research question. In the end, the experts were asked to read the transcription of their interviews for accuracy and validation.

For understanding literature in general, it is worthwhile to consider the work of Roman Jakobson, a member of the Russian Formalism school in the early twentieth century. Originally published in Russian in 1921 by Jakobson and translated from Russian to English by Edward J. Brown in 1973, Jakobson (1973) explained that "the subject of literary scholarship is not literature but literariness (literaturnost), that is, that which makes of a given work a work of literature" (p. 62). The essence of literariness is defamiliarization. "The primary aim of literature…is to estrange or defamiliarize…by disrupting the modes of ordinary linguistic discourse, literature 'makes strange' the world of everyday perception and renews the reader's lost capacity for fresh sensation" (Abrams & Harpham, 2015, p. 142). Kathy Torabi (2010) elaborated, "Defamiliarization causes the audience to confront the object on a different level, elevating and transforming it from something ordinary or practical into work that is considered art" (n.p.). For ASL literature, it is appropriate to expect that literariness and defamiliarization take place with signed language just as it is for spoken languages. As such, ASL students have the opportunity of experiencing a form of art when watching an accomplished signer performing on the videotape.

Because the scholarly study of ASL literature is relatively young, establishing a list of criteria to create the canonicity of ASL literary works has only recently been discussed but not yet agreed to as a community. Since the publication of Cynthia Peters' *Deaf American Literature: From Carnival to the Canon* in 2000, Sutton-Spence and Kaneko (2016) appear to be the first to discuss the concept of canon (or canons) explicitly and in depth related to signed language literature, especially folklore. The authors provide definitions for, respectively, general canons of folklore and a signed language canon of folklore. The definition of the former is "collections that are generally accepted as being representative, and are understood to be central examples of folklore, judged 'the best' by a community" (p. 40). As for the latter's definition, "[it] is made up of the sign language folklore that is judged to be the knowledge that is most valued by community members as their folklore" (p. 40). In spite of the authors' acknowledgment that the last definition is incomplete and that people frequently dispute who has the authority to determine what is canonical and what is not, they state that Stephen Ryan's 1993 article entitled *Let's Tell an ASL Story* suggested that all canonical stories in signed language possess particular elements in common. The elements are as follows:

- Show the deaf perspective.
- Inform us in some way about the concerns of the deaf community and its relationship with the hearing world.
- Increase signing skills (including for second language learners).
- Increase cultural sensitivity.
- Teach cultural values.
- Be good entertainment. (Spence-Sutton & Kaneko, 2016, pp. 40-41)

Ryan's article discussed ASL storytelling techniques, activities, and resources, as well as suggestions for effective storytelling without making reference to the term canon or canons. Sutton-Spence and Kaneko perceived Ryan's stories as canonical, but the criteria that the authors developed based on Ryan's article appear to be ambiguous and inadequate. They do not seem as comprehensive as suggested in the newly-created definition for ASL literature by the author of this paper (see pages 65-66). This new definition could be used as a starting point for canon formation for ASL literature.

In terms of the different literatures of the world, forming a canon is no easy task due to the varying and disputed perspectives. The definitions of a canon range from the simplest to the most detailed. A simple definition is "a collection of key works of literature" (Wilczek, 2012, p. 1687). M. H. Abrams and Geoffrey Harpham (2015) provide a detailed definition:

> The canon is the result of the concurrence of a great many (often unexpressed) norms and standards, and among these, one crucial factor has been the high intellectual and artistic quality of the canonical works themselves and their attested power to enlighten, give delight, and appeal to widely shared human concerns and values. (p. 45)

It is reasonable to expect that some of the works of ASL literature have the capacity of becoming canonical. This paper's focus is on understanding ASL literature in more basic terms. ASL literature has a number of issues that have not been addressed until now. The issues addressed here center around the handling of: (1) the so-called ASL literary works that have ties to English,

(2) many definitions for ASL literature in current use, and (3) the confusion associated with works that arise out of the deaf community as a collective as opposed to works that are authored by individual performers. A particular problem that this paper will address is how ASL literature is widely taught to hearing students while such instruction is either non-existent or marginal when it comes to deaf students in American and Canadian schools. Perhaps the most challenging aspect of ASL literature lies in the fact that it is not written. Some students taking ASL classes are perplexed by the idea that signed language has a literature when there are no books to read. Clearly, a reaffirming support for the concept of oral literature is needed. While many ASL instructors are culturally deaf and accustomed to the narration of stories and poems delivered in ASL 'through the air,' they need to defend teaching ASL literature in its unique form.

The Relationship between Oral Literature and ASL Literature

In Ben Bahan's paper entitled *ASL Literature: Inside the Story*, he asks, "Can there be a literature that is not written down?" (1992, p. 153). The significance of this question cannot be downplayed. Bahan is a Professor in the Department of American Sign Language and Deaf Studies at Gallaudet University, a premier institution of higher education for deaf students in Washington, D.C. He is deaf and an accomplished storyteller in his own language, ASL. He has a long resume of traveling throughout the United States and abroad to give storytelling performances on stage. His most recent work is entitled *Bleeva* (2014), which is best described as a monologue with insight and humor on why deaf people are here on earth. Audiences of Bahan's performances over the years have been both deaf and hearing with the important understanding that they know ASL (S. Supalla & Bahan, 1994a, 1994b). Individuals who pay admission have been eager to be entertained by Bahan's performances, thus, the audience experience has to be significant, including that of a literary nature.

One reason Bahan raised the question of whether there can be a literature that is not written down has to do with the conventional attitude that literature is tied to the written form. As a matter of fact, there are opposing positions among scholars on this issue. While some scholars such as Walter Ong believe that there is no such thing as oral literature, others such as Isidore Okpewho think differently. Ong (1982) views oral literature as a "strictly preposterous term" because it has "nothing to do with writing at all" (p. 11). He then adds, "Thinking of oral tradition or a heritage of oral performance, genres and styles as 'oral literature' is rather like thinking of horses as automobiles without wheels" (p. 12). Okpewho (1992) believes that there can be a literature that is not written down. He defines oral literature as "literature delivered by word of mouth" or as "those utterances, whether spoken, recited or sung, whose composition and performance exhibit to an appreciable degree the artistic characteristics of accurate observation, vivid imagination and ingenious expression" (pp. 3-5).

Even though the term 'oral literature' is perceived as oxymoronic, it is now becoming accepted as a term, mostly as a result of an increasing number of publications in recent years (see Burns, 2011; Halpern & Miller, 2014; Niles, 2010; Okpewho, 1992; Reichi, 2016; Turin, Wheeler, & Wilkinson, 2013). There is a website called World Oral Literature Project "to document and make accessible endangered oral literatures before they disappear without record" (University of Cambridge Museum of Archaeology and Anthropology, 2015, n.p.). As stated by the website entitled Ethnologue: Languages of the World, there are 6,909 living languages in the world (Lewis, 2009). No systematic way of gathering data on the specific number of unwritten languages is available today (Robinson & Gadelii, 2003). However, several sources refer to the overwhelming number of unwritten languages. Ong (1982, 2009) believes that, out of approximately 3,000 spoken languages in the world today, about 2,922 languages are oral. Another source indicates that, out of 5,000 or more languages, roughly 500 have a written tradition (Kenrick, 2000). Examples of spoken languages that have no written form are Abom (a language of Papua, New Guinea), Alabama (a Native American language of the United States), Assiniboine (an Aboriginal language of Canada), and Reli (a language of India) (University of Cambridge Museum of Archaeology and Anthropology, 2015, n.p.). These languages have a rich literature of their own.

During the time when awareness that ASL is a bona fide human language was still emerging, colleges and universities around the country struggled over whether ASL could be taught as a foreign language for credit on a par with French or Spanish, for example. The lack of written literature for the signed language was viewed as a serious obstacle and was used as an argument against the offering of ASL coursework. Nancy Frishberg (1988) who is hearing and knows ASL felt obligated to write a scholarly article to respond to such resistance. She wrote that "the case can be made by analogy with the greatest traditions in Western and non-Western literature that written forms of language are not required for a community to possess a well-formed aesthetic in poetry, narrative, humor, and rhetoric" (p. 150). The classical Greek Odyssey was used as an example for how it was delivered orally long before it was written down. The important point that Frishberg made lies in how the Odyssey was originally created in the oral form. This suggests that literature being limited to the written form is too narrow.

While the situation for ASL literature has now improved, there is one important observation to consider. Gallaudet University professor, Lois Bragg (1993), who is deaf, pointed out that "ASL…is an 'oral' language – perhaps the only true living 'oral' literature in the western world" (p. 416). It appears that a new dimension to the foreign language learning experience has taken place with students studying ASL. They are not only learning a new language, but that it is part of an oral culture that deaf people have cultivated and maintained right here in the United States and Canada.

ASL has its share of misunderstandings as a human language, including how it was once thought to be lacking linguistic properties and is rather made up of rudimentary gestures or is even a code of English. Language has been narrowly defined as spoken, not signed (Meier, 2002). Deaf people suffered the consequences of social stigma against their language. Signed language was widely forbidden from use in American and Canadian schools for the deaf during the latter part of the nineteenth century and for most of the twentieth century (see Van Cleve & Crouch, 1989 for the historical review of deaf education). Spoken language bias is a serious matter and only recently has it become a subject of scholarly scrutiny. It is hoped that this attention will lead to a long deserved provision of quality education for deaf students (Cripps & S. Supalla, 2012).

Should there be bias associated with literature, it would be about literature having to be written. The dominant nature of written culture in the western world at present is a serious matter. Any person who does not know how to read and write is widely viewed as problematic. Bahan (1992) wrote on behalf of the deaf community and ASL as follows:

> The issue of whether literature needs to be written in order to be literature is a question of power, not merit. Literature can indeed be either oral or written. What we need to do is find a way to explicate and demonstrate the literary value of our oral tales. In order to do that, Bahan and [S.] Supalla . . . in their ASL Literature Series . . . have analyzed their narratives, Bird of a Different Feather and For a

Decent Living. Each narrative has been divided into structural units and analyzed to show how both narratives conform to the tradition of oral literature. (p. 155)

Thanks to video technology, the narratives included in the ASL Literature Series were broken down into lines, stanzas, and other parts so that they could be better studied in a classroom where ASL is taught as a foreign language. Students are now able to locate a particular part of the narrative based on the use of stanza numbers and view it again for comprehension or where a particular event occurs that is critical to answering a literary question (S. Supalla & Bahan, 1994a; 1994b). Both videotaped narratives *Bird of a Different Feather* and *For a Decent Living* allow students to view them at their convenience without having to see the performers in a live performance, for example.

The narratives for the ASL Literature Series are single-authored works (see Rose, 1994 for further discussion on the emergence of the authorship concept for ASL as a non-written language). Bahan created the first narrative while Sam Supalla authored the second narrative. Since its release in 1994, the ASL Literature Series enjoys widespread circulation among the ASL and Deaf Studies programs that purchase it for use in the classroom. The description of these narratives in The Super Store of Books, Media and Equipment for the Deaf (2016-2017) is as follows:

"Bird of a Different Feather is about a bird born into a family of eagles. The response to this family member parallels the experiences of many deaf children born into hearing families" (p. 36).

"For a Decent Living relates the challenges and adventures of a deaf boy who leaves his hearing family in search of his own identity as a deaf person" (p. 36).

Based on the wording above, Bahan's narrative as an allegorical fable would be correct in describing such work. S. Supalla's work is best characterized as a novella. Deaf identity is one theme among many in ASL literature. Bahan and S. Supalla's narratives incorporate the fact that a vast majority of deaf children are born to hearing parents who do not know signed language (at least initially; e.g., Lederberg, Schick, & Spencer, 2013). While some deaf children are born to deaf parents who use ASL and are raised in the deaf community, they are few in proportion. The majority of deaf children have to find their own ways of assimilating into the deaf community (Erting & Kuntze, 2008). Understandably, the unique and complicated identity development experiences so prevalent for deaf people can make a good story.

At the same time, not all single-authored works are tied to ASL literature. There are works that are folkloristic or community-owned with no known source of their origins (Bahan, 1992, 2006; Krentz, 2006; Rose, 1994). Frequently, these works were created and shared at the schools for the deaf, at banquets and other organized events that the deaf community hosted, and in homes (Peters, 2000). These works were narrated to entertain and instruct the young generation and to pass on the values and perspectives that deaf people possess. The enduring power of folklore centers on its amusement and educative function for the deaf community, and it can be seen as a mirror of deaf culture (Rutherford, 1993). A well-known example is the story of *The Hitchhiker*, which involves a driver who was deaf and picked up a hearing hitchhiker. The hearing hitchhiker was not only dumbfounded at the fact that a deaf person could drive, but also tried to trick him with something, but was outsmarted at the end. The noted discrimination associated with how deaf people should not drive was effectively addressed in the folklore, and deaf individuals have come to love and cherish the story. The fact that the deaf person was driving in the story serves as a reminder to deaf people that the right to drive was a hard-fought victory according to the historical accounts.

In comparison to the narratives in the ASL Literature Series, *The Hitchhiker* is older with its origins tracing back at least to the time when automobiles were first introduced in the United States and Canada. Carol Padden and Tom Humphries (1988) who are deaf scholars reported on a folktale that has been passed down over hundreds of years in France. The French deaf community shared with them a story of how a hearing priest, the Abbé de l'Epée was 'lost in the world' until the time he encountered two deaf girls. This incident is what led to the founding of the world's first public school for the deaf, and the girls' signing went on to become what is now known as French Sign Language. The impact as told in the story is not limited to France as its model of deaf education was duplicated in the United States and Canada leading to the rise of ASL. The significance of the French story is best presented by Padden and Humphries as follows:

> We finally realized that the story is not about the Abbé de l'Epée. Instead it has come to symbolize, in its retelling through the centuries, the transition from a world in which deaf people live alone or in small isolated communities to a world in which they have a rich community and language. This is not merely a historical tale, but also a folktale about the origin of a people and their language. Epée's movement from the darkness of the night into the light and warmth of the house of the deaf girls is entirely appropriate as a central image in a folktale of origins, not at all unlike folktales of other cultures. (p. 29)

With the recent rise of single-authored works in ASL, one cannot help but wonder about this occurrence in light of the folklore tradition in the deaf community. One possible explanation lies in the deaf community's response to a change in society where ASL instruction started becoming a fixture in academia. This is where financial opportunities become real with thousands of hearing students taking ASL courses each year. Thus, deaf individuals who had a high level of literary skills made the decision to videotape themselves and market their work. Bahan and S. Supalla are good examples, but it is important to note that they continue to do live performances to this day. Hearing individuals who are signers and talented performers jumped in as well. One example is the video production that came out *Tomorrow Dad Will Still Be Deaf and Other Stories* by Bonnie Kraft (1997), who was born to deaf parents, has native signing skills and a strong affiliation with deaf culture.

The impact of video technology must also be noted, for it allows performers to view themselves on the videotape to make changes or improvements until the 'final version' has been created (Rose, 1994). Single-authored works in ASL are oral and require memorization just like folklore in the deaf community but may have slight variances from performance to performance, but any work that is videotaped is preserved for posterity. A narrative in the folklore tradition can be changed as it passed from one individual to another. The main idea might remain the same, but any individual can add or delete a segment or expand or de-emphasize an idea. In contrast, once a narrative is recorded on videotape, changes do not occur and the narrative remains the same in the eyes of the audience. The individual who performs professionally is more focused on form or the structure of the work, rather than only on the content matter.

This is where the delivery of *Bird of a Different Feather* and *For a Decent Living* becomes important as the performers had their distinctive and eloquent styles at play. The same appears to be true for other single-authored works in ASL. This does not mean that *The Hitchhiker* is obsolete as it continues to have its own value and function. For one thing, folklore allows anybody to tell or re-tell a piece while it is a different matter for a single-authored work (as it would be difficult to duplicate and needs to be studied for how it is told artistically). Should there be a study of ASL folklore, students will need to have the opportunity to view different versions of *The Hitchhiker* through videotape for study. This is where the students will learn that a narrative may vary (among signers) yet preserve itself at the same time, which is crucial for understanding the nature of the folklore tradition in general.

A Comprehensive Definition for ASL Literature

At this point, it becomes clear that ASL literature is real. The fact that ASL literature is subject to scholarly study and publications through articles and books (e.g., Bahan, 1992; Bauman, Nelson, & Rose, 2006; Brueggemann, 2009; Byrne, 1996; Christie & Wilkins, 1997; Frishberg, 1988; Kuntze, 1993; Lane et al., 1996; Marsh, 1999; Ormsby, 1995; Peters, 2000; Rose, 1992, 1994; S. Supalla & Bahan, 1994a, 1994b; Valli et al., 2011) is encouraging. Rose (1994, p. 155) explained that "[a]s ASL literature joins the canon of world literature, scholars and artists need to ensure that this literature in a visual-spatial mode establishes its own criteria for what constitutes quality". A comprehensive definition would thus be a good start. Of particular importance is the issue that there are some ASL works on the market that appear to be of questionable quality and misrepresent deaf culture (S. Supalla, 2006). There are seven known definitions of ASL literature developed by scholars and they are in need of a critical review. The definitions are as follow:

Table 1
Existing Definitions of ASL Literature

Sources	Existing Definitions of ASL Literature
Byrne (1996, p. 49)	The term 'ASL literature' includes not only stories in ASL but also ASL poetry, riddles, [humor], and other genres of a 'through the air' literary tradition. ASL literature is not English literature translated into ASL but is comprised of original compositions that have arisen from the thoughts, emotions, and experiences of culturally [d]eaf people, and have been passed on by 'hand' (through ASL) from one generation to another.
Christie & Wilkins (1997, p. 58)	Like most languages without a written form, ASL has a literature that has been passed down and shared within generations in a face-to-face manner. And like most languages having a rich 'oral' literary tradition, the storytellers/poets of ASL have a respected and leading role in the nurturing and growth of ASL literature. According to [Peter] Cook, the basic ingredients of ASL literature include not only the building blocks and grammar of ASL, but also miming and gestures that exploit the visual medium. Thus, in much the same way that the poetry of nonsigned languages use sound play and rhyme, ASL poetry uses visual play and sign rhymes.

Gibson (2000, pp. 9-10)	ASL has a literature of its own that has been passed down from one generation to the next by culturally [d]eaf people. It is conveyed in a visual-spatial dimension. It shares similar elements and functions of any literature in any language. For [d]eaf children, it is an important building block that presents them with opportunities to learn language, knowledge, values, morals, and experiences of the world around them. It also provides them with the bridge to English and other literatures. ASL Literature exists in two forms; 1) through the air and 2) on videotapes.
Gibson & Blanchard (2010, p. 24)	ASL has a literature of its own that has been passed down from generation to generation by the ASL community. It shares similar elements and functions of any literature in any language. For children that use ASL, it is an important foundation that presents them with language, heritage, and experiences of the world around them. ASL also provides them with a bridge to English and other literatures. ASL literature exists in two formats: live and on video.
Marsh (1999, p. 269)	[The definition of ASL literature is] signed expressions of enduring interest.
Peters (2001, p. 130)	[V]ernacular ASL literature is more of an 'art for a people's sake' than an 'art for art's sake.' The literature in the vernacular is largely a collective, 'orally' (via sign language) transmitted body of performative works. Although ASL works are increasingly recorded or even composed on videotape, many [d]eaf American storytellers, like the storytellers of old, still travel about and render stories and other vernacular art forms to comparatively small groups of people, frequently as part of some occasion such as a social gathering, ceremony, or festival. Drawing on a traditional stock of stories and other ASL art forms, an ASL artist can choose a story, art form, or even an original piece by another ASL artist, make individual modifications, and, at one time or another and in front of one or another group of viewers, render his or her own variant. An ASL storyteller, in telling a story to a group of viewers, does not just recite but performs to keep the interest and attention of the viewers, enacting one or more characters in a kind of semi-play, semi-mime, all the while conveying mannerisms, appearances, attitudes, and emotions.
Rose (1992, p. 26)	ASL literature refers to texts <u>created in ASL</u> by [d]eaf people, whether the pre-videotape folklore forms or the new body of single-authored works preserved on videotape.

The multiple ASL literature definitions listed above have produced a number of insights, but some require clarifications. One example is the description of ASL literature as vernacular as it relates to Bahan's telling of *Bird of a Different Feather* on the stage as opposed to its videotaped edition. Bahan has done the same narrative in both settings. To be sure, there may be some variations when he performed the narrative on different occasions or from stage to stage, but the quality is consistently high, in the opinion of the author in this paper. Moreover, the videotaped edition renders at least one version permanent. He is likely to have viewed himself when making the videotape to make sure that all segments are presented in their best version but it does not mean that the narrative being told live or on the stage would be inferior as Peters' definition implies. While *The Hitchhiker* may use vernacular language, the negative connotation of this term suggests that it should be avoided altogether.

When looking through all the definitions, there seems to be a strong emphasis on ASL literature being transmitted through generations. That may be true concerning the folklore type of literature, but not so with the single-authored type. *Bird of a Different Feather* serves as a good example of a work of ASL literature that is rather new and not subject to transmission across generations. A better definition is needed that will encompass works of ASL literature that are not necessarily passed through generations.

There is one definition suggesting that only deaf individuals can contribute to ASL literature, which is not correct. The exemplary work of Bonnie Kraft cannot be discarded because she can hear. Theoretically, a hearing signer has the capacity of performing high quality literary work with the important understanding that this person respects deaf culture (S. Supalla, 2006). Another example is the possession of native signing skills and avoidance of taking the role of a deaf person, especially with that of a character with his/her point of view for the entire work. Although deaf individuals are not specified in any of the definitions discussed thus far, they are expected to respect their own culture as well.

The need for a comprehensive definition of ASL literature is evident, especially with how varied the current descriptions are. Also, the descriptions are not comprehensive enough to capture the heart of ASL literature. While one definition mentions "enduring interest" as an important attribute for what characterizes ASL literature, which is correct, this attribute is not included in the other definitions. The fact that Byrne's definition in 1996 mentions that literary works done originally in a language other than ASL should not be treated as something that is integral to ASL literature is an interesting proposition.

With all of these different considerations, it is necessary to return to the author's doctoral dissertation, where an initial version of a comprehensive definition of ASL literature was put together. The ASL and Deaf Studies experts who participated in the dissertation research were asked to peruse the definitions and share their perspectives as to whether these definitions were comprehensive enough to completely represent all of ASL literature. The first version was included in the dissertation, but more changes were made during the writing of this paper. The additional analysis done with the seven definitions that were published prior to the dissertation work require those changes. This new definition has the potential to assist scholars, educators, and performers to have an enhanced understanding of what ASL literature is and is not. Also, the definition could possibly assist in creating, developing, and using quality materials for ASL literature classes in K–12 and post-secondary settings. The new definition of ASL literature is constructed as follows:

> ASL literature is defined as a body of published American and Canadian works in video format that are both folkloristic and single-authored. It has literary elements and functions that can be found in literatures of different languages both unwritten and written. The genres include poetry, drama, and prose including humor, riddles, and allegories. ASL literature comprises original compositions that have arisen from the thoughts, emotions, and experiences of native signers using the linguistic structures and features of ASL. It includes the ability to decipher, organize,

construct, and present literary works effectively, imaginatively, and eloquently. Every work should comprise literary devices (e.g., rhyme, rhythm, imagery, and style), correct ASL language (e.g., word production, grammar, and non-manual signals), aesthetics (e.g., innovative and complex yet simple, highly cohesive, and delight inducing), and ASL socio-cultural aspects (e.g., authenticity of native signers' experiences, thoughts, and emotions). At the same time, differences between the folkloristic and single-authored works must be noted for the former emphasizes content whereas the latter expands to include on the structure of the work. The benefits of ASL literature include the literary experience appreciated with an enduring interest in the visual and gestural modality and how it applies to all individuals.

The Question of Translation

One may wonder why originality matters for ASL literature. What is wrong with those works translated from English? In the Canadian province of Ontario, ASL literature is subject to integration into the curriculum for use in schools for the deaf. A teacher who is employed at one of these schools, Linda Wall, made this important observation: "Original ASL stories and poetry convey the experiences and emotions of ASL culture" (Miller, 2008, n.p.). The term ASL culture may not be widely used in the literature, but this teacher was trying to make the point that the literature is tied to the language. Heather Gibson who leads the curriculum work at the Ontario provincial schools for the deaf provided an explanation for why originality is important and why English-to-ASL translations should be avoided:

> [L]iterary works are intimately tied to the culture from which they spring and have their deepest meaning and strongest impact when the storyteller and audience share a common cultural ground. Previously, poetry, songs and stories were translated from English to ASL. Deaf Cinderella is a classic example. This translated curriculum never fully resonated with [ASL-using deaf] children because it came from an experience foreign to them. It would be like an anglophone learning English only through translations of French literature. (Miller, 2008, n.p.)

The ASL and Deaf Studies experts interviewed in the author's doctoral dissertation provided their perspectives on English-to-ASL translations. One expert was adamant about the oppressive nature of translation and how languages ought to be separated when it comes to literature. Another expert ironically commented, "To translate a book from English to ASL is easier than creating an original ASL literary work. [This is why] there are so many translated works out there".

The translation issues that arise in ASL literature occur in other languages. Because of linguistic and cultural differences and complexities, not every work can be appropriately and accurately translated. For example, "poems, [humor], puns, a play between different linguistic registers or vocabulary, stylistic qualities, multi-levels of meaning, connotations, imagery, and culturally specific allusion" cannot be translated (Finnegan, 1992, p. 178). Sapir (1921, p. 237) states the following:

Language is the medium of literature as marble or bronze or clay are the materials of the sculptor. Since every language has its distinctive peculiarities, the innate formal limitations – and possibilities – of one literature are never quite the same as those of another. The literature fashioned out of the form and substance of a language has the color and the texture of its matrix. The literary artist may never be conscious of just how he is hindered or helped or otherwise guided by the matrix, but when it is a question of translating his work into another language, the nature of the original matrix manifests itself at once. All his effects have been calculated, or intuitively felt, with reference to the formal "genius" of his own language; they cannot be carried over without loss or modification.

Interestingly, a majority of ASL and Deaf Studies experts interviewed in the author's doctoral dissertation believe that English-influenced rhymes of poetry (e.g., alphabetical handshape or ABC stories, worded handshape or name stories, and initialized handshape) should not be part of ASL literature. One reasoned that, for these rhymes, "the language of origin is English." This is followed with the statement that "the production and use of handshapes is awkward because the handshapes do not follow ASL rules". Another commented, "ABC stories are a bastardized form of ASL and English". Another explained the motivation related to English-influenced rhymes, especially alphabetical handshape rhyme:

[Administrators and educators] in deaf education always feel the need to connect [deaf] children to English culture. How do they do that? Through assimilation. It occurs when they make an attempt to internalize [deaf] children with [English] literature.

One of the ASL and Deaf Studies experts who objected to the motivation behind the English-influenced rhymes recalled a conversation she had with a deaf ASL poet who enlightened her about the relevance of ASL rhymes as follows:

I asked him why he had never created English-influenced handshape rhymes. He reservedly shook his head and gave no explanation for it. However, he explained a bit that he would like to challenge [us] to create poems using closed handshape rhyme, open handshape rhyme, double handshape rhyme, movement rhyme, location rhyme, palm orientation rhyme, non-manual signal rhyme, and handedness rhyme [which are entirely ASL]. I sensed from conversing with him that, as compared to the English-influenced rhymes, deaf children could easily connect to these rhymes because they are naturally embedded with their own [signed language-based] culture.

Translating works from English to ASL is acceptable as long as they are categorized as English literature, not ASL literature. For example, Sign Media, Inc., a video producing company in the United States, created a DVD set of *Sherlock Holmes Mysteries*, which includes *The Adventure of the Blue Carbuncle*, *The Adventure of the Speckled Band*, and *The Adventure of the Red-Headed League*. Originally published in English and translated into ASL, the set should be catalogued under the genre of mysteries under English literature. The same holds true for original works written in English by deaf or hearing writers about deaf people and their life experiences.

For example, originally written by Douglas Bullard, *Islay* is a novel about a deaf man who wishes to turn an imaginary island into a state populated by deaf people. This novel should be placed under the genre of novels under English literature (Byrne, 2013).

This explains, in part, why a comprehensive ASL literature definition needs to take into account the concept of linguistic accessibility. The fact that ASL is a signed language has ramifications for how deaf children are best taught rhymes during the kindergarten year, for example. Rhymes or language play must be in the signed language modality, and there are several works published and made available for purchase (e.g., *The ASL Parent-Child Mother Goose Program: American Sign Language Rhymes, Rhythms, and Stories for Parents and their Children* by the Ontario Cultural Society of the Deaf, 2004). What has been done in deaf education has been incorrectly based on English rather than on ASL (see S. Supalla & Cripps, 2008 for further discussion on the linguistic accessibility concept). Deaf children need to be introduced to an alphabet that represents ASL, ideally through the handshape, location, and movement parameters that underline the formation of words in ASL. The ASL-phabet is one writing system that has been developed to address the deficiencies in the design of deaf education (see S. Supalla & Blackburn, 2003 and S. Supalla & Cripps, 2011 for more information on the accessible curriculum design for use with deaf children).

The Taxonomy of ASL Literary Genres

The discussion now moves on to what genres exist in ASL literature. There are hundreds of published ASL literary works that are in need of organization. Initiated by S. Supalla (2001), The University of Arizona ASL Literature Collection comprised of folklore, originals, and translations in both VHS and DVD formats serves as a testimony to the explosion of ASL literary works since the 1980s. The collection includes rare published works in ASL prior to the 1980s. The earliest known recordings of works of ASL literature date back to 1910 when the National Association of the Deaf (NAD) began a project of creating twenty-two films of master signers giving a variety of performances. One of the films which is frequently referred to today is *Preservation of the Sign Language* from 1913 (Sign Media, Inc., 1997). In this piece, then-President of the NAD, George Veditz, delivers powerful rhetoric in ASL criticizing the banishing of signed language from deaf education that was underway at that time. While Veditz was himself deaf, the NAD film collection includes a hearing signer by the name of Edward Miner Gallaudet who was President of Gallaudet University at the time. He was born to a deaf mother, which explains how he became a native signer. Mr. Gallaudet did an ASL translation of a story written in English.

The University of Arizona Literature Collection also includes other filmed ASL performances from 1925 to 1940. Charles Krauel, a deaf filmmaker, took a visual record of deaf community events and some literary performances given by skillful signers (T. Supalla, 1991, 1994). The signed performances in Krauel's films were subject to cataloguing in the ASL literature collection along with many more that are contemporary. Some of the contemporary examples belong to Sign Media, Inc. This company developed and released a videotape of original poems and narratives in ASL entitled *American Sign Language: Tales from the Green Books* in 1980. A decade later, the same company produced a series of videotapes called *Poetry in Motion* featuring three ASL poets named Clayton Valli, Patrick Graybill, and Debbie Rennie. Another company that followed in the release of ASL literary works at a great volume is DawnSignPress.

Prior to 1980, only a small number of ASL works were available and these were frequently translations of English-language works. While the University of Arizona Collection may be extensive, its organization needs further improvements. The collection has a weakness when it comes to genres. The author's doctoral dissertation includes input from ASL and Deaf Studies experts who offered ideas regarding how to best organize ASL literature. Not only was the interview helpful, the dissertation includes a literature review that includes various experts who expressed more ideas in scholarly publications (e.g., Bahan, 2006; Bauman et al., 2006; Brueggemann, 2009; Byrne, 1997–2012; Lane et al., 1996; Peters, 2000; Rose, 1992; Rutherford, 1993; S. Supalla, 2001; Valli, 1993; Valli et al., 2011). The dissertation is where all original ASL works were placed under appropriate genres, sub-genres, and sub-sub-genres.

As seen in Figure 1, ASL literature comprising single-authored works is divided into three main genres: poetry, drama, and prose. The folkloristic works stand as a genre that is coequal to the single-authored works. The folkloristic sub-genres are legends, tall tales, riddles, and humor.

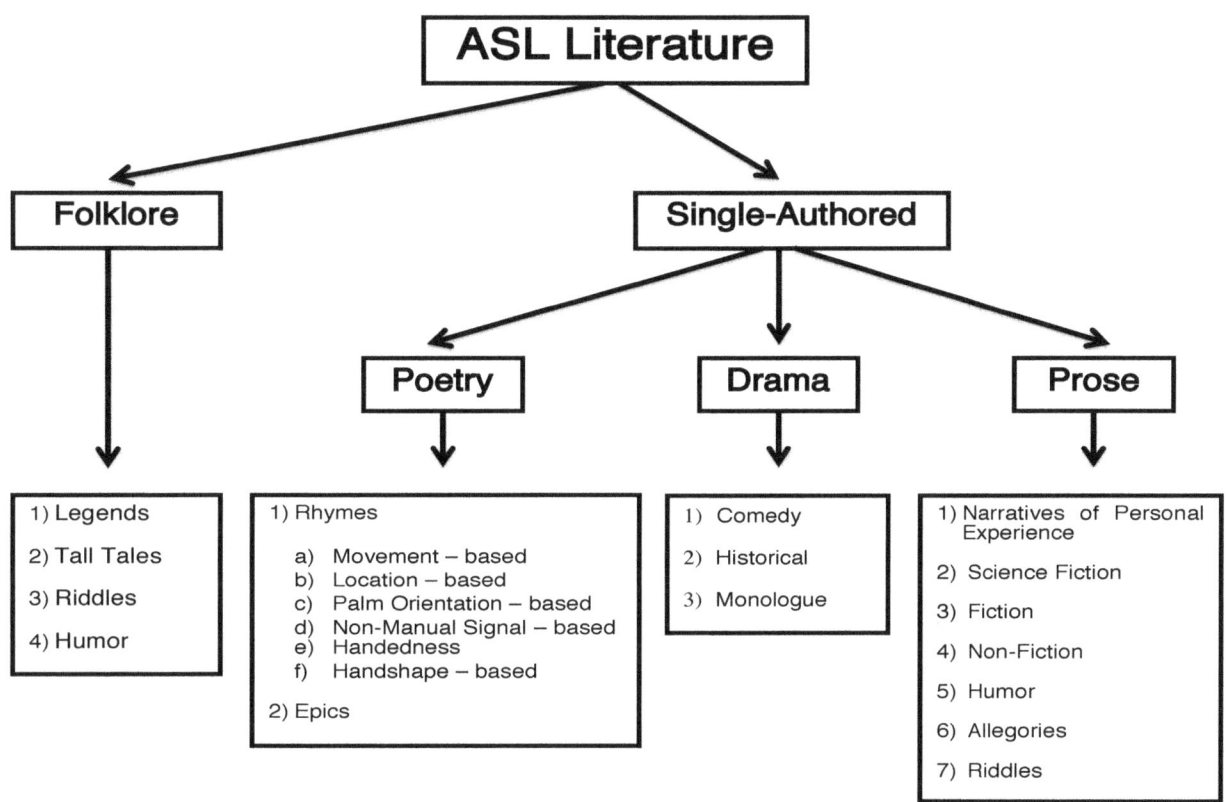

Figure 1
Genres of ASL Literature

As part of the re-organized taxonomy for ASL literature, works listed in the original University of Arizona Collection that were translations from English were subject to removal. Other improvements to the collection included correction of bibliographical errors and additions of newer original ASL works. The revised collection has been renamed *A Database of ASL*

Literature for Use in the United States and Canada. The database is expected to serve as a resource for scholars, educators, performers, and all other interested parties and individuals to have easy and quick access to ASL literature for recreational, pedagogical, and scholarly purposes. There are a total of 443 single-authored works captured in VHS, DVD, and online publications. Of these 443 works, 81 are works of poetry, 15 are works of drama, and 347 are works of prose. The total number of folkloristic works is 41.

Discussion

As evident in this paper, the taxonomy of genres legitimizes various works as ASL literature. The same holds true for the number of published ASL literary works, which are in the hundreds although the number is lower for certain sub-genres. For example, the prose genre has only one known allegorical work for ASL (which is Bahan's *Bird of a Different Feather*). The same holds true for the riddle category (which is David Burke's *Run*). While the dramatic growth of ASL literature over the last few decades confirms a large number for the whole body of works, the database still needs more works.

The removal of works of translation from the database puts an emphasis on works that authentically originate in ASL. However, the present database will need to be subject to more stringent review based on the comprehensive definition of ASL literature set forth in this paper. Some single-authored works may be removed from the database due to their poor representation of deaf culture, due to the poor language skills of the performer, or due to a lack of literary devices. Occurrences of these deficiencies are expected to be rare, however. Even the ASL literature definition may be subject to modifications to better represent the body of ASL literary works. What is important is that there are now established parameters for what can be called a work of ASL literature.

For future research, it is important to explore the question of canonicity for ASL literature. Such a project will help further our understanding of what constitutes quality in ASL literary works. Despite the large number of literary works in the database, it is possible to narrow down to a small number that stand out for study and appreciation (see Bloom, 1994; Brown, 2010; Harris, 1991; Ungureanu, 2011; Wilczek, 2012 for further discussion on how canonicity is pursued for a given language's literary works). For now, very little is known about what makes an ASL literary work exceptional. Yet, there are quite a few performers or smooth signers who "can weave a story so smoothly that even complex utterances appear simple, yet beautiful" (Bahan, 2006, p. 24). Padden and Humphries (2005) make no direct reference to the ASL Literature Series of Ben Bahan's *Bird of a Different Feather* and Sam Supalla's *For a Decent Living* as canonical but they praise the storytellers for establishing a standard for ASL literary works. They write:

> Gradually the poetry and the performances of equally inventive and skilled ASL storytellers like Sam Supalla and Ben Bahan became a new standard for public performance, showing that ASL should become the name of the language of the community, because it had such rich potential. (p. 137)

There are two possible approaches for an ASL literary work to be admitted to canonicity. One is to develop a list of canonical qualities to determine which work is canonical and which is not. The ASL Literature Series and other works by exemplary ASL poets such as Clayton Valli and Ella Mae Lentz should serve as a benchmark for what is to be included in the canon. Another approach is via the creation of a pedagogical canon in which individual colleges or universities develop a concrete list of reading texts for each course. "The wider pedagogical canon is made up of the most frequently taught texts, a list that is empirically verifiable" (Gallagher, 2001, p. 54).

In addition, Guillory (1995) explains that a canonical work in a spoken language is reproduced for, and used by generations of readers. At the present time, there is no evidence that the ASL Literature Series and the works by Valli and Lentz are incorporated into syllabi and consistently taught to generations of students in American and Canadian colleges and universities that offer programs in ASL and/or Deaf Studies. A study could be put together to examine whether ASL literary works such as the ASL Literature Series and the works of Valli and Lentz, which were published close to 30 years ago, have been consistently used and taught in ASL and/or Deaf studies courses in the period since their publication (the equivalent of one generation).

Conclusion

In this paper, four main topics have been discussed and reframed for a better and clearer understanding of what constitutes ASL literature. The present status of ASL literature is fairly strong. We are a far cry from the time when Nancy Frishberg scrambled in the 1980s to convince the American and Canadian academia about the vitality of oral literature and that ASL has literary capacity. Not only does the comprehensive ASL literature definition in this paper support the legitimacy and quality of the literary language of the deaf community, it serves as a benchmark for the additions to come in the future. A consideration of how ASL literature should best be taught in schools for the deaf will need to be part of this important undertaking. Accomplished ASL performers will need to share their input as well. General knowledge of ASL literature, through familiarity with the works listed in the database as well as critical and theoretical analyses, ASL teaching experience, and native fluency in ASL, can support the task of creating a canon of ASL literature.

References

Abrams, M. H., & Harpham, G. G. (2015). *A glossary of literary terms* (11th ed.). Stamford, CT: Cengage Learning.

Bahan, B. (1992). ASL literature: Inside the story. In J. Cebe (Ed.), *Deaf studies: What's up?: 1991 conference proceedings* (pp. 153–164). Washington, DC: Gallaudet University, College for Continuing Education.

Bahan, B. (2006). Face-to-face tradition in the American deaf community. In H-D. L. Bauman, J. L. Nelson, & H. M. Rose (Eds.), *Signing the body poetic: Essays on American Sign Language literature* (pp. 21–50). Berkeley, CA: University of California Press.

Bahan, B. (2014). *Bleeva: A narrative of our existence.* Presented at the 6th Biennial Deaf Studies Today! Conference in Orem, UT on Saturday, April 12, 2014. Retrieved from https://www.uvu.edu/asl/dst/docs/Bleeva%20-%20DST%202014.pdf

Bauman, H-D. L., Nelson, J. L., & Rose, H. M. (Eds.). (2006). *Signing the body poetic: Essays on American Sign Language literature.* Berkeley, CA: University of California Press.

Bloom, H. (1994). *The western canon: The books and school of the ages.* New York, NY: Riverhead Books.

Bragg, L. (1993). Deafness and orality: An electronic conversation. *Oral Tradition, 8*(2), 413-437.

Brown, J. L. (2010). Constructing our pedagogical canons. *Pedagogy, 10*(3), 535-553.

Brueggemann, B. J. (2009). *Deaf subjects: Between identities and places.* New York, NY: New York University Press.

Burns, A. F. (2011). *An epoch of miracles: Oral literature of the Yucatec Maya.* Austin, TX: University of Texas Press.

Byrne, A. (1996). ASL storytelling to deaf children: "MORE! MORE! MORE!" In D. Smith & A. Small (Eds.), *Teacher research in a bilingual bicultural school for Deaf students* (pp. 49–62). Toronto, ON: Queen's Printer for Ontario.

Byrne, A. (1997–2012). *ASL literature genres and sub-genres.* Unpublished manuscript, E. C. Drury School for the Deaf, Milton, ON, & Lamar University, Beaumont, TX.

Byrne, A. P. J. (2013). *American Sign Language (ASL) literacy and ASL literature: A critical appraisal* (Unpublished doctoral dissertation). York University, Toronto, ON.

Christie, K., & Wilkins, D. M. (1997). A feast for the eyes: ASL literacy and ASL literature. *Journal of Deaf Studies and Deaf Education, 2*(1), 57–59.

Cripps, J. H., & Supalla, S. J. (2012). The power of spoken language in schools and deaf students who sign. *International Journal of Humanities and Social Science, 2*(16), 86-102.

Erting, C. J., & Kuntze, M. (2008). Language socialization in deaf communities. In P. Duff and N. H. Hornberger (Eds.), *Encyclopedia of language and education* (2nd ed., Vol. 8, pp. 287-300). New York, NY: Springer Science + Business Media, LLC.

Finnegan, R. (1992). *Oral traditions and the verbal arts: A guide to research practices.* New York, NY: Routledge.

Frishberg, N. (1988). Signers of tales: The case for literary status of an unwritten language. *Sign Language Studies, 59*, 149–170.

Furman, N., Goldberg, D., & Lusin, N. (2010). *Enrollments in languages other than English in United States institutions of higher education, fall 2009.* New York, NY: The Modern Language Association of America.

Gallagher, S. V. (2001). Contingencies and intersections: The formation of pedagogical canons. *Pedagogy: Critical Approaches to Teaching Literature, Language, Composition, and Culture, 1*(1), 53-67.

Gibson, H. (2000, March). American Sign Language curriculum: A GOLDEN KEY! *OCSD Bulletin, 6*(3), 9–11.

Gibson, H., & Blanchard, N. T. (2010). The linguistics and use of American Sign Language. *Canadian Journal of Education of the Deaf and Hard of Hearing, 1*(1), 22–27.

Goldberg, D., Looney, D., & Lusin, N. (2015). *Enrollments in languages other than English in United States institutions of higher education, fall 2013.* New York, NY: The Modern Language Association of America.

Guillory, J. (1995). Canon. In F. Lentriccia & T. McLaughlin (Eds.), *Critical terms for literary study* (pp. 233-249). Chicago, IL: University of Chicago Press.

Halpern, A. M., & Miller, A. (2014). *Stories from Quechan oral literature.* Cambridge, UK: Open Book Publishers.

Harris, W. V. (1991). Canonicity. *Publications of the Modern Language Association of America (PMLA), 106*(1), 110-121.

Humphries, T., & Padden, C. (2004). *Learning American Sign Language: Levels I & II – beginning & intermediate* (2nd ed.). Boston, MA: Pearson Education, Inc.

Jakobson, R. (1973). Modern Russian poetry: Velimir Khlebnikov [Excerpts]. In E. J. Brown (Ed.), *Major Soviet writers: Essays in criticism* (pp. 58-82). New York, NY: Oxford University Press.

Kenrick, D. (2000). Towards a typology of unwritten languages. In T. Acton & M. Dalphinis (Eds.), *Language, blacks and gypsies: Languages without a written tradition and their role in education* (pp. 24–31). London, England: Whiting & Birch.

Kraft, B. (1997). *Tomorrow dad will still be deaf & other stories* [DVD]. San Diego, CA: DawnSignPress.

Krentz, C. B. (2006). The camera as printing press: How film has influenced ASL literature. In H-D. L. Bauman, J. L. Nelson, & H. M. Rose (Eds.), *Signing the body poetic: Essays on American Sign Language literature* (pp. 51–70). Berkeley, CA: University of California Press.

Kuntze, M. (1993). Developing students' literary skills in ASL. In B. D. Snider (Ed.), *Post Milan ASL & English literacy: Issues, trends, & research* (pp. 267–281). Washington, DC: Gallaudet University, Continuing Education and Outreach.

Ladd, P. (2003). *Understanding deaf culture: In search of deafhood.* Tonawanda, NY: Multilingual Matters Ltd.

Lane, H., Hoffmeister, R., & Bahan, B. (1996). *A journey into the DEAF-WORLD.* San Diego, CA: DawnSignPress.

Lane, H., Pillard, R. C., & Hedberg, U. (2011). *The people of the eye: Deaf ethnicity and ancestry.* New York, NY: Oxford University Press.

Lederberg, A. R., Schick, B., & Spencer, P. E. (2013). Language and literacy development of deaf and hard-of-hearing children: Successes and challenges. *Developmental Psychology, 49*, 15-30.

Lewis, M. (Ed.). (2009). *Ethnologue: Languages of the world* (16th ed.). Dallas, TX: SIL International. Retrieved from http://www.ethnologue.com/

Marsh, C. E. (1999). ASL literature. In J. Cebe (Ed.), *Deaf studies VI: Making the connection: 1999 conference proceedings* (pp. 269–276). Washington, DC: Gallaudet University, College of Continuing Education.

McQuillan, J. (2012). *The most studied, fastest growing, and "best represented" languages in U.S. colleges.* Retrieved from http://backseatlinguist.com/blog/the-most-studied-fastest-growing-and-best-represented-languages-in-u-s-colleges/

Meier, R. P. (2002). Why different, why the same? Explaining effects and non-effects of modality upon linguistic structure in sign and speech. In R. P. Meier, K. Cormier, & D. Quinto-Pozos (Eds.), *Modality and structure in signed and spoken languages* (pp. 1-25). New York, NY: Cambridge University Press.

Miller, L. (2008, September). Exemplary teacher: Principal Heather Gibson: Taking pride and making strides in ASL culture and curriculum. *Professionally Speaking: The Magazine of the Ontario College of Teachers.* Retrieved from http://professionallyspeaking.oct.ca/september_2008/exemplary.asp

Niles, J. D. (2010). *Homo narrans: The poetics and anthropology of oral literature.* Philadelphia, PA: University of Pennsylvania Press.

Okpewho, I. (1992). *African oral literature: Backgrounds, character, and continuity.* Bloomington, IN: Indiana University Press.

Ong, W. J. (1982). *Orality and literacy: The technologizing of the word.* New York, NY: Methuen.

Ong, W. J. (2009). The orality of language. In S. D. Blum (Ed.), *Making sense of language: Readings in culture and communication* (pp. 45–51). New York, NY: Oxford University Press.

Ontario Cultural Society of the Deaf. (2004). *The ASL parent-child mother goose program: American Sign Language rhymes, rhythms, and stories for parents and their children* [DVD]. Mississauga, ON: Ontario Cultural Society of the Deaf.

Ormsby, A. (1995). Poetic cohesion in American Sign Language: Valli's 'Snowflake' and Coleridge's 'Frost at Midnight.' *Sign Language Studies, 88*, 227-244.

Padden, C. (1980). The deaf community and the culture of deaf people. In C. Baker & R. Battison (Eds.), *Sign language and the deaf community: Essays in honor of William C. Stokoe* (pp. 89-103). Silver Spring, MD: National Association of the Deaf.

Padden, C., & Humphries, T. (1988). *Deaf in America: Voices from a culture.* Cambridge, MA: Harvard University Press.

Padden, C., & Humphries, T. (2005). *Inside deaf culture.* Cambridge, MA: Harvard University Press.

Peters, C. L. (2000). *Deaf American literature: From carnival to the canon.* Washington, DC: Gallaudet University Press.

Peters, C. L. (2001). Rathskellar: Some oral-traditional and not-so-traditional characteristics of ASL literature. In L. Bragg (Ed.), *Deaf world: A historical reader and primary sourcebook* (pp. 129–146). New York, NY: New York University Press.

Reichi, K. (Ed.). (2016). *Medieval oral literature.* Boston, MA: Walter De Gruyter, Inc.

Robinson, C., & Gadelii, K. (2003). *Writing unwritten languages.* Retrieved from http://portal.unesco.org/education/en/ev.php-URL_ID=28300&URL_DO=DO_TOPIC&URL_SECTION=201.html

Rose, H. M. (1992). *A critical methodology for analyzing American Sign Language literature* (Unpublished doctoral dissertation). Arizona State University, Phoenix, AZ.

Rose, H. M. (1994). Stylistic features in American Sign Language literature. *Text and Performance Quarterly, 14*, 144–157.

Rutherford, S. (1993). *A study of American deaf folklore.* Burtonsville, MD: Linstok Press.

Ryan, S. (1993). Let's tell an ASL story. In J. Mann (Ed.), *Deaf studies III: Bridging cultures in the 21st century: 1993 conference proceedings* (pp. 145–150). Washington, DC: Gallaudet University, College for Continuing Education.

Sandler, W., & Lillo-Martin, D. (2006). *Sign language and linguistic universals.* New York, NY: Cambridge University Press.

Sapir, E. (1921). *Language: An introduction to the study of speech*. New York, NY: Harcourt, Brace.

Sign Media, Inc. (Distributor). (1997). *The preservation of American Sign Language: The complete historical collection* [DVD]. Available from http://store.signmedia.com/1668.html

Smith, C., Lentz, E. M., & Mikos, K. (2008). *Signing naturally: Student workbook – units 1 – 6*. San Diego, CA: DawnSignPress.

Stokoe, W. C. (Ed.). (1980). *Sign and culture: A reader for students of American Sign Language*. Silver Spring, MD: Linstok Press.

Supalla, S. (2001). *The University of Arizona ASL literature collection*. Unpublished manuscript, Sign Language/Deaf Studies, University of Arizona, Tucson.

Supalla, S. (2006). *Future of American Sign Language literature*. Presented at the 2nd Biennial Deaf Studies Today! Conference in Orem, UT (April 6 – 8, 2006).

Supalla, S., & Bahan, B. (1994a). *ASL literature series: Bird of a different feather & for a decent living: Student workbook*. San Diego, CA: DawnSignPress.

Supalla, S., & Bahan, B. (1994b). *ASL literature series: Bird of a different feather & for a decent living: Teacher's guide*. San Diego, CA: DawnSignPress.

Supalla, S., & Blackburn, L. (2003). Learning how to read and bypassing sound. *Odyssey, 5*(1), 50-55.

Supalla, S. J., & Cripps, J. H. (2008). Linguistic accessibility and deaf children. In B. Spolsky & F. M. Hult (Eds.), *The handbook of educational linguistics* (pp. 174-191). Malden, MA: Wiley-Blackwell.

Supalla, S. J., & Cripps, J. H. (2011). Toward universal design in reading instruction. *Bilingual Basics, 12*(2).

Supalla, T. (1991). Deaf folklife film collection project. *Sign Language Studies, 70*, 73-82.

Supalla, T. (1994). *Charles Krauel: A profile of a deaf filmmaker* [VHS]. San Diego, CA: DawnSignPress.

Sutton-Spence, R., & Kaneko, M. (2016). *Introducing sign language literature: Folklore and creativity*. London, UK: Palgrave.

The Super Store of Books, Media and Equipment for the Deaf. (2016-2017). *ASL literature series* [Books & DVD]. Eden Prairie, MN: Harris Communications. Retrieved from http://www.harriscomm.com/asl-literature-series-bird-of-a-different-feather-book-dvd-student-set.html

Torabi, K. (2010). *The art of defamiliarization.* Retrieved from http://english638. blogspot.com /2010/02/art-of-defamiliarization.html

Turin, M., Wheeler, C., & Wilkinson, E. (Eds.). (2013). *Oral literature in the digital age: Archiving orality and connecting with communities.* Cambridge, UK: Open Book Publishers.

Ungureanu, D. (2011). What to do about constructing the literary canon: Canonicity and canonical criteria. In L. Papadima, D. Damrosch, & T. D'haen (Eds.), *The canonical debate today: Crossing disciplinary and cultural boundaries* (pp. 87-98). New York, NY: Rodopi.

University of Cambridge Museum of Archaeology and Anthropology. (2015). *World oral literature project.* Retrieved from http://www.oralliterature.org/

Valli, C. (1993). *Poetics of American Sign Language poetry* (Unpublished doctoral dissertation). Union Institute, Cincinnati, OH.

Valli, C., Lucas, C., Mulrooney, K. J., & Villanueva, M. (2011). *Linguistics of American Sign Language: An introduction* (5th ed.). Washington, DC: Gallaudet University Press.

Van Cleve, J. V., & Crouch, B. A. (1989). *A place of their own: Creating the deaf community in America.* Washington, DC: Gallaudet University Press.

Wilcox, S. E. (Ed.). (1989). *American deaf culture: An anthology.* Silver Spring, MD: Linstok Press.

Wilczek, P. (2012). The literary canon and translation: Polish culture as a case study. *Sarmatian Review, 32*(3), 1687-1692.

Zinza, J. E. (2006). *Master ASL! – Level one.* Burtonsville, MD: Sign Media, Inc.

Understanding Signed Music

Jody H. Cripps
Towson University

Ely Lyonblum
University of Toronto

Abstract

The existence of music performances rooted in American Sign Language (ASL) and deaf culture indicates that music is not exclusive to the audible domain. Terminologies such as "deaf music" and "visual music" as used in the literature are subject to discussion and clarification. Theory, roles of language, culture, and music and their relationships to each other become important for exploratory investigation regarding what music means to deaf people. As a result, signed music is the term deemed most appropriate to define the original lyric and/or non-lyric musical performances done by native deaf signers. This is different from English-to-ASL translation of songs that may be a common practice at present. Unlike translated songs, signed music performances are originally developed within the signed modality. Signed music frequently includes deaf experiences and is fully accessible. A review of a study on the work of two deaf performers demonstrates how signed music constitutes a unique form of performance art, yet shares elements that are common to music in general. This paper is intended to generate a greater interest among scholars and researchers on the topic of signed music, and expand the scope of signed language performance art.

Introduction

"I see little of more importance to the future of our country and of civilization than full recognition of the place of the artist. If art is to nourish the roots of our culture, society must set the artist free to follow his [or her] vision wherever it takes him [or her]."

- John F. Kennedy, 35th President of the United States

The concept of signed music is new and exciting by all accounts, but at present, the definition of music is far from clear to the deaf community. While deaf people are known for signing or using American Sign Language (ASL), they have frequently struggled with talking about music, especially about the possibility of a form of music that is enjoyable and authentic to their experience. While there are indications that signed music has been around for some time, only in recent years has it experienced a growth with increasing sophistication. While terms such as "deaf music" and "visual/eye music" are used in the literature, the term "signed music" is most accurate. The reasons for this are explained below. One must ask: What does signed music encompass? Is deaf music just another term for signed music? In addition, music is conventionally perceived as primarily an auditory phenomenon. Yet original musical performances created by deaf performers are a real phenomenon, and very much misunderstood at this point in time (J. H. Cripps, Small, Rosenblum, S. Supalla, Whyte, & J. S. Cripps, in press).

The aim of this article is to generate a greater understanding of signed music as an art form. This includes taking note that watching original musical performances through hand and body movements appears to be enjoyable and authentic for deaf people. A review of the study published on two deaf performers serves as the basis for the existence of signed music and how it compares to what is known for music in general. Also included in the study is the consideration of signed music incorporating the deaf experience. While there is some discussion of deaf people's musical experiences in the literature, and about the concept of visual music outside the deaf community, some clarification is needed. This includes explaining why the term *signed music* appears to be the appropriate term used to describe the musical phenomenon that is created within the deaf community. For this paper, it is necessary to start by defining the key properties that constitute music. Language and culture play significant roles in creating and shaping musical performances that can be applied to deaf people and their music.

Language, Culture, and Music

For this paper, a simple diagram of what constitutes music is critical for understanding signed music. The interwoven relationship between language, culture, and music must be appreciated as a universal phenomenon concerning human beings. Figure 1 illustrates how language interacts with culture and culture with music. Language has a relationship with music as evident through the production of lyrics. Non-lyrics do not include language in an explicit manner, but musicians who produce these sounds are expected to possess the necessary language and cultural knowledge. This explains the "broken" line between language and music concerning non-lyrics.

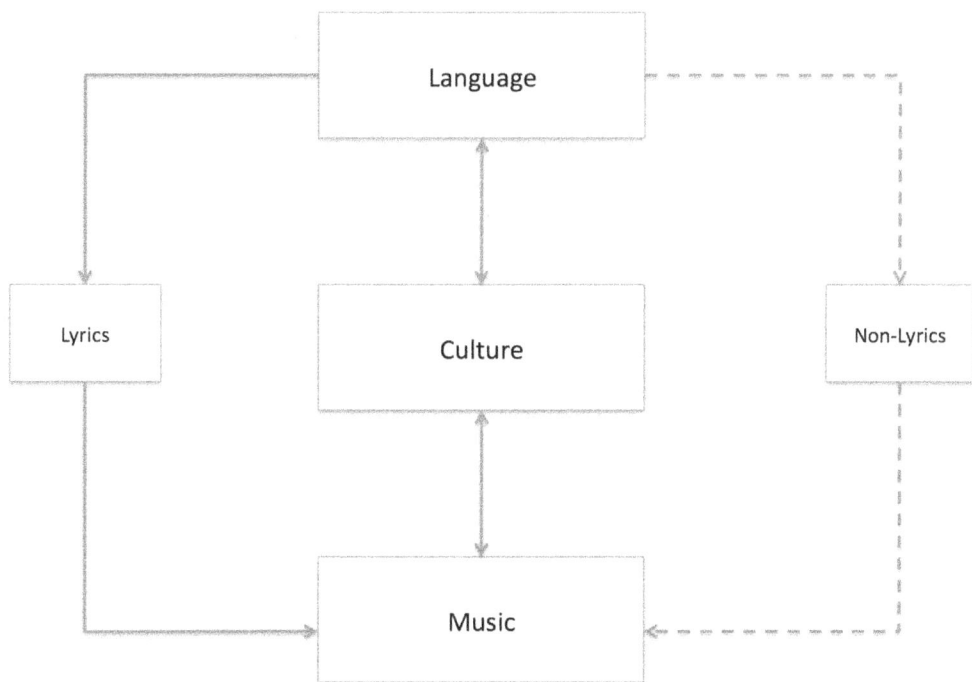

Figure 1: Music's Ties to Language and Culture Through the Production of Lyrics and Non-Lyrics

Readers will learn this paper represents a different point of view on what constitutes music. With this in mind, this section has three topics for discussion: 1) ASL and deaf culture as the basis for signed music, 2) background on music and deaf people, and 3) the place of signed music in music theory.

ASL and Deaf Culture

Music is a universal experience for human beings, and deaf people cannot continue to be excluded from this experience. Individuals who are deaf since birth, for example, may not have the opportunity to hear and enjoy music in the traditional sense, but they can appreciate a parallel experience known as signed music. Signed music is real and meaningful to the person who knows ASL. The recognition of ASL as a full-fledged human language has been supported through linguistic research over the last several decades (see Meier, 2002 for a historical review of ASL research). In the United States and parts of Canada, ASL was formed and used by deaf people who are primary signers.[1] ASL is part of the human language family and shares linguistic properties as reported for spoken languages (Sandler & Lillo-Martin, 2006; Stokoe, 1960; Valli, Lucas, Mulrooney, & Villanueva, 2011; also see Bergman & Wallin, 1990; Sutton-Spence & Woll, 1999; Zeshan, 2000 for similar analysis on the linguistic principles for Swedish Signed Language, British Sign Language, and Indo-Pakistan Sign Language).

Both signed languages and spoken languages are known for having five linguistic properties: phonology, morphology, syntax, semantics and pragmatics (Akmajian, Demers, Farmer, & Harnish, 2010). All of these properties are found in the lyrical component of signed music, suggesting that signed music uses ASL as its linguistic basis. With non-lyrics, one must also be receptive to the idea of a signer performing abstract hand movements without any signed words in use. The hand movements would be visually analogous to sound and need to be perceptually enjoyable by following the general principles of how music works (see Padden & Humphries, 1988 for a similar discussion regarding hand movements in ASL poems that resemble sound). The popular perception that ASL is a soundless language (e.g., Petitto, Langdon, Stone, Andriola, Kartheiser, & Cochran, 2016) requires response. Traugott and Pratt (1980) stated that "each language, indeed each sub-variety of a language, has its own unique 'sound,' yet the number of possible sound distinctions that can be made in any language is quite limited, and all languages share at least some sets of sounds" (p. 41).

The reality of signed music centers on an interwoven relationship of language and culture and culture with music concerning deaf people. Supporting this, Saville-Troike (2003) affirmed that "there is no doubt … that there is a correlation between the form and content of a language and the beliefs, values, and needs present in the culture of its speakers" (p. 28). Similarly, Brown (1994) pointed out that "[a] language is part of culture and a culture is part of a language; the two are intricately interwoven so that one cannot separate the two without losing the significance of either language or culture" (p. 165). Kramsch (1998) further elaborated on how language is used in a culture as described, "When [language] is used in contexts of communication, it is bound up with culture in multiple and complex ways" (p. 3). This kind of paradigm led to comments from scholars like Padden (1980) and Rutherford (1988), who asserted that American deaf people have their own culture based on two important sources. First, they have their own signed language:

---

[1] The description of deaf people as primary users of ASL distinguishes them from hearing people who may know and use signed language. Signing hearing individuals enjoy access to both ASL and spoken language(s). Individuals who are deaf since birth or become deaf before the age of two may not have the auditory experience of learning and internalizing English or any other spoken language. Accessibility is a key issue regarding how ASL becomes the primary language for deaf people (see S. Supalla & J. H. Cripps, 2008 for the concept of linguistic accessibility).

ASL. Second, deaf people share similar cultural properties as found in other cultures. Thus, signed music cannot be written off and should be considered seriously.

Yerker Andersson, a Deaf Studies scholar, rightly notes that "[signed] language is at the core, embodying terminology issues and the role and use of language in the development of cultural identity" (Andersson & Burch, 2010, pp. 193-194). It is important to remember that the discussion to this point is regarding deaf people who know ASL and reside in North America. Nanda & Warms (2002) explained that languages reflect cultural emphases and create the ways in which cultures categorize their physical and social environment including the ideas, objects, or relationships. In other words, languages and cultures interact and dynamically impact each other, and the formation of different languages in the world exemplifies the distinction between cultures. It is not surprising that deaf people in different geographic areas have different cultures which are reflected in their indigenous signed languages (Padden, 2010). For example, New Zealand Sign Language used by culturally deaf New Zealanders may include signed words reflecting perspectives and experiences (cuisine, clothing, etc.) that are not part of the deaf American experience. The impact of different cultures on signed music is expected to be immense, especially regarding the prospect of how musical experiences vary among deaf people around the world. The basic idea that deaf people have their own music through non-audible sources is revolutionary in its own right.

Music and Deaf People

The perspective of hearing people on the history of deaf people's capacity for creating and enjoying music is best described as "harsh." The fact that deaf people were once viewed as lacking language (and sufficient cultural knowledge; e.g., Bender, 1981; Branson & Miller, 1998; Van Cleve & Crouch, 1989) would negate any discussion on the concept of signed music. Speaking and the use of spoken language were thought to be the norm, thus deaf individuals were expected to suffer the consequences. This scenario emphasizes that deaf people are 'forever' detached from musical experiences. Hollywood films and English literature depicting deaf people have reinforced the view that deaf people lead a dreary life in silence (Padden & Humphries, 1988; Schuchman, 1988). However, it is important to note that the American deaf community is known for being closely knit and resilient over the years (which include ethnic-like qualities; Lane, Pillard, & Hedberg, 2011). Culturally deaf people frequently see themselves as 'us' and hearing people as 'them', for example. The oppressive history experienced by deaf people (i.e., not allowed to sign in school, limited employment opportunities, poor education, and their disability poorly received) is well-documented (e.g., Baynton, 1993, 1996; Bruch, 2004; Gannon, 1981; Lane, 1984, 1999; Moores, 1996; Van Cleve & Crouch, 1989).

The fact that deaf people are well-known for being signers is remarkable given their unfavorable history with society. In the beginning of deaf education, during the early nineteenth century, the situation was considered positive. Policies were supportive of ASL, and the establishment of schools for the deaf allowed deaf children from a wide territory to assemble and socialize for the first time. The critical mass of deaf children growing up together led to the creation of strong local and nationwide deaf communities when they reach adulthood. While the situation for ASL worsened over time during the early 1900s, deaf people simply went underground for the maintenance of their language and for functioning as signers (Van Cleve & Crouch, 1989). The modern situation with ASL and deaf culture continues to be challenging with many deaf children integrated in local public schools. This has resulted in the deterioration of socialization opportunities with signed language, and decreased exposure to native signing peers and adults (e.g., J. H. Cripps & S. Supalla, 2012; see Van Cleve, 1993 for further discussion on the society's damaging assimilationist attitudes associated with the integration efforts).

With this background, signed music has remained viable by all accounts. The well-known Deaf Studies scholar, Benjamin Bahan (2006) reported on a particular type of song that has been performed in the American deaf community for a long time. The percussion songs, as they are called, were conducted entirely through visual means and some were documented and preserved in film (e.g., T. Supalla, 1994). Some other forms of signed music such as *Rescue at the Sea* (an ensemble song) can be seen in the widely acclaimed *My Third Eye* production of the National Theatre of the Deaf (1973), Mary Beth Miller's *Mexican Cowboy* (1991), and finally, David Supalla's *A Ballad of the USA Flag* (C. Supalla & D. Supalla, 1991).

At the same time, deaf individuals who are fluent in ASL and part of deaf culture have frequently accepted the notion that music belongs to hearing people. Society's perceptions that deaf people are associated with silence, and that music is reserved to the audible form, clearly has created an impact on the deaf community's consciousness about music in general. Yet, according to the first author who is a member of the deaf community, deaf people have complained about how offensive it is for a hearing person to say that he or she would miss music the most upon experiencing hearing loss. It appears hearing people are outright ignorant about the possibility that deaf people have enjoyed their own kind of music all along. It can be said that signed music sorely lacks formal recognition (as occurred with ASL as the language of deaf people not being recognized for most of the history up to the 1970s and 1980s).

Last, deaf people have mixed feelings about the recent trends in how 'music' has been brought to their attention. There is a dramatic rise in translated English-to-ASL songs from hearing signers and translators who believe that they are helping deaf people listen to music performances (J. H. Cripps et al., in press). Perhaps internet technology has prompted many hearing translators to sign while listening to a song more than ever. A large number of translated music performances can be found online through YouTube or Vimeo (Leigh, Andrews, & Harris, 2016; Maler, 2015). In terms of quality, translated songs are frequently presented using ASL grammatical structure, movement or rhythm of the signs. These works can look weak, especially if the translator struggles with timing trying to produce musical ASL within the time constraints of songs in English. While deaf people watch a music translation performance, they often find it difficult to say that they have enjoyed the performance.[2] This outcome is justified when one thinks carefully about how the translated performances are difficult to follow based on different cultural knowledge and experiences between hearing and deaf people (J. H. Cripps et al., in press).

Music Theory Receptive to Signed Music

In the literature from the fields of ethnomusicology and cultural musicology, music is contextualized through its deep-rooted roles within culture. What has been discussed for deaf culture (with ASL playing a central role) supports the concept of signed music. The reported history associated with signed music (and contemporary deaf musicians subject to elaboration later

---

[2] Many songs with lyrics are not really about the words; the lyrics may represent a more symbolic meaning. The interpretation of auditory lyrics is up to the hearing listener. When song lyrics are translated into ASL, the interpretation of the meaning is created by the interpreter/translator, and not left to the deaf listener. Thus, the opportunity for the listener to "interpret" the musical experience does not parallel the auditory experience and may or may not reflect the original idea of the writer.

in this paper) also falls in line with how scholars have written that every culture in the past and present has its own music regardless of size (Brown, Merker, & Wallin, 2000; Hamm, Nettl, & Byrnside, 1975). However, music theory acceptance of signed music is a rather recent phenomenon. The relationship between culture and music may have existed for thousands of years, but the topic of connecting culture to music remains new to music scholarship. A book called *The Cultural Study of Music* was published in 2003 and its second edition, published in 2012, documents one of the earliest times when ethnomusicologists with similar interests came together to further investigate the relationship between culture and music across disciplines. The idea that deaf people have their own music will reinforce what has been discussed for ethnomusicology and cultural musicology. The ASL signing deaf community in the United States and Canada is vulnerable to society's biases and discriminatory practices, and opportunities for music over the years has been restricted (especially since signed music has been excluded from, or not even considered for, curricula in schools for deaf children).

Music has been categorized by scholars into Western and non-Western arts. This division was formalized throughout the late 19th and early 20th centuries. Classical music is considered part of Western art music, and is the foundation of traditional musicology. Ethnomusicologists concentrate on other types of music, (e.g., jazz, rap, pop rock, etc.) which are considered the roots of non-Western culture. During the 1980s and 1990s, musicologists, music theorists, and ethnomusicologists studied new types of music, then considered a radical shift from classical to a broader perspective on music in academia (Middleton, 2012). These new types of music included perspectives across the arts, humanities and social sciences. Middleton (2012), one of these music scholars, experienced obstacles when he argued that culture has a role in music, thus music scholars must think differently than before, by including culture. *Music Studies* is the new approach that he proposed to define this particular "culture and music" paradigm. Cook (2008) also recommended that musicologists broaden their horizons by including a range of different disciplines such as ethnomusicology, historical musicology, and music psychology. With this approach, music scholars are now more receptive to the idea of music as part of culture, as they have begun analyzing music for its meaning beyond a strictly theoretical perspective.

This approach also gave way to Cultural Musicology, the analysis and criticism of works in American and Western European Music through cultural studies. The formation of Music Studies has essentially opened the doors for investigations in signed music as its subgenre (J. H. Cripps, Rosenblum, Small, & S. Supalla, 2017). To sum it up, when asked "who does music belong to?," the second author of this paper, a music scholar, clarified in his interview that "[music] belongs to whatever culture it comes from" (Canadian Cultural Society of the Deaf, 2015, p. 5). Thus, it is appropriate to state that signed music belongs to deaf culture and deaf people themselves.

One of many research interests from ethnomusicologists is to examine how cultural meaning is captured through musical performance. With this kind of investigation, audiences and performers' cultural identities can be further analyzed to understand how identity plays an important role in creating performances (Cook, 2012). That is, the performer and audience who share cultural identities are likely to appreciate the same musical performances due to similar experiences and perspectives. Deaf people, may share cultural identities through discrimination. An example of similar experiences that deaf people faced is "audism" and it is expressed in some contemporary signed music performances (J. H. Cripps et al., 2017). This term expresses discriminatory behavior toward deaf people due to their inability to hear, and suggests the superiority of spoken language when compared to signed language (Bauman, 2004; Eckert &

Rowley, 2013; Humphries, 1977; Lane, 1999; also see J. H. Cripps & S. Supalla 2012 for how spoken language bias is a serious social problem worldwide). J. H. Cripps et al. (in press) observed that deaf performers with strong cultural identity are the ones who create culturally appropriate music performances through the signed modality.

To define music in a broader sense, Thaut (2005) noted that music is a highly abstract and non-representational art that demonstrates human thought, feelings, and sense of movement. Kramer (2003) argued that music is frequently perceived as lacking representational-semantic richness. Specifically, he stated that individuals must understand the music's "cultural meaning [even] with the lack of referential destiny found in [musical] words or images" in order to appreciate the music performance (p. 127). Theoretically, the same claim is likely to be made for signed music through the necessary investigation with deaf community members.

Cook (2000) also claimed that music is embedded within social contexts. Music has five basic elements: rhythm, timbre, texture, melody, and harmony. All of these elements are identified in Western music, whereas non-Western music does not require all elements to be present. Melody and harmony are two elements that are not so easily distinguishable in non-Western forms of music (Schmidt-Jones, 2007). How these elements are used in signed music as promoted in the United States and Canada is wide open for creative interpretation. The key definitions for each of five musical elements are synthesized and listed as:

- Rhythm: the repetitive pulse of the music or a rhythmic pattern that is repeated throughout the music,
- Timbre: all of the aspects of musical sound that are not based upon the sound's pitch, loudness, or length (e.g., a flute and oboe play the same note, but they have distinctive sonic qualities),
- Melody: a series of notes (of particular pitch and duration) together, one after the other,
- Texture: the overall qualities in the music at any given moment […] containing many or few layers, and
- Harmony: multiple pitches sounding at a time, which interact with the melody. (Schmidt-Jones, 2007, pp. 71-83 as cited in J. H. Cripps et al., 2017, p. 5)

In addition to these elements, the broadest feature of music is motif. Drabkin (2004) defined this feature as:

a short musical idea – melodic, harmonic, rhythmic, or any combination of these three. [It] may be of any size, and is most commonly regarded as the shortest subdivision of a theme or phrase that still maintains its identity as an idea. (n.p.)

Signed music offers many challenges for research and scholarship, particularly when it comes to the motif and the five musical elements discussed here. These contribute to the aesthetics of any signed music work. New ideas uncovered regarding signed music through research and scholarship will contribute to the understanding of this new subgenre in Music Studies. The impact on the deaf community and society is expected to be significant given the long history of misconceptions associated with music and deaf people. The notion of lyrics and non-lyrics being real through signed music comes with the validation for an even greater universality of music as prevalent through ASL and deaf culture.

A Demonstration of Signed Music

Attention now shifts to understanding how two contemporary culturally deaf performers created music that is enjoyable and entirely visual through both lyrics and non-lyrics. This is made possible through references to the case study published by J. H. Cripps et al. (2017) on the music performances produced by the performers. The researchers relied on the ethnomusicological approach to examine the first performance, *Eyes* by Janis E. Cripps (https://www.youtube.com/watch?v=YnwJsFHFebg) and *An Experiment Clip* by Pamela Witcher (https://www.youtube.com/watch?v=zPHraTb36wc). Thick description (Geertz, 1973) and comparative analysis were two methods that the researchers used. Three different clips for each performance were targeted for the use of musical elements, linguistic principles, and media formats. Each of the clips was described using thick description format. Data from both performances were then compared as part of comparative analysis. The findings are substantial and important. Based on the analysis of *Eyes* and *An Experiment Clip*, there are analogues to the music properties, with the evidence of rhythm, timbre, and texture as well as motif. Although more work is needed with other signed music works in the near future, *Eyes* and *An Experiment Clip* align with the non-Western version of music (due to the absence of melody and harmony).

Through the researchers' analysis of the two performers' work, it became clear that their musical pieces incorporated deaf people's experiences reflecting the perspectives in deaf culture. For example, in J. E. Cripps' piece, she began her song by looking closely at her hands as if they had special value for the production of ASL. She also expressed the value of her eyes for the perception of her language as well. The motif of water-like movement with series of rhythmic variations can be seen in J. E. Cripps' piece, and the reference to the water has a significant meaning. The music cannot be easily produced in the water, but the visual version of the music is readily expressed through her use of hands and movements. The message in response to audism is quite clear. Music is not limited to the audible sense as promoted by society at large.

For the purpose of this paper, only the description of how lyrics and non-lyrics occurred in signed music is provided. This is part of confirming signed music's following through the framework on music's ties to language and culture through the production of lyrics and non-lyrics as discussed in the preceding section. One clip from *An Experiment Clip* and the other from *Eyes* are provided for viewing follow:

Video 1: Experimental Clip
https://youtu.be/8Ttxu_UhCHA

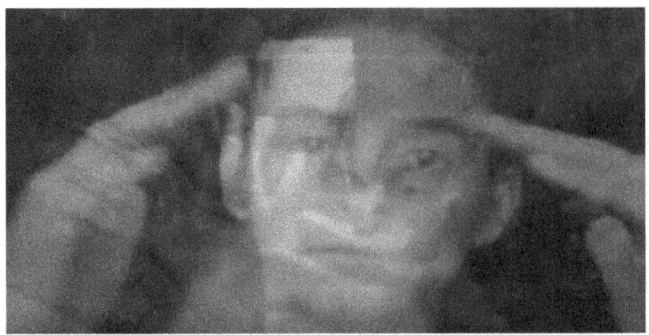

Video 2: Eyes
https://youtu.be/BjTX0X5zGVs

The distinction between lyrics and non-lyrics can be identified with the two signed music clips under consideration here. *An Experiment Clip* has incorporated the wordings of ASL, which suggests a direct relationship between language and music for deaf people. Witcher's piece entails the use of language that is similar to what is generally known as "[t]he words of a song in a 'musical' or of a popular 20th-century song" (Kennedy, Kennedy, & Rutherford-Johnson, 2012, p. 513). Signed words in sentences are included in ASL phrases such as "it is nice to meet you." In contrast, *Eyes* is non-lyric with J. E. Cripps' avoidance of signs representing specific words. She performed using hand and facial movements in an abstract way. J. E. Cripps successfully produced what is visually perceived as music from beginning to end. Such outcome includes the use of signed notes, which is proposed as analogous to the audible musical notes.

Some Clarifications

While signed music has been the term used throughout this paper, another term to identify music performances by deaf people also exists. In both literature and in the labeling of published signed music pieces, *deaf music* is a widely used term. Loeffler (2014) and Leigh et al. (2016) used the term "deaf music" to represent the art of deaf performers who perform auditory-centric music, which does not characterize the definition of signed music as presented in this paper. In both Loeffler's article and Leigh et al.'s book, the understanding of what music really means to deaf people appears to be limited. Of particular concern is how deaf musicians listed in Leigh et al. are influenced by the auditory tradition of music as follows:

> The Wild Zappers, founded in 1989, combines ASL, music, and dance to promote cultural and educational awareness of sign[ed] language and [d]eaf people. There are deaf jazz singers (Mandy Harvey), deaf bands (Beethoven's Nightmare), opera singers (Janine Roebuck), and solo percussionists (Dame Evelyn Glennie) (Lammle, 2010). There are also deaf rappers and groups, such as Prinz-D, Warren "Wawa" Snipe, DJ Supalee, Sho'Roc, Signmark, and Sean Forbes (Peisner, 2013) (as cited in Leigh et al., 2016, p. 249).

A large number of hearing performers have attempted to translate various English music pieces into ASL with the naive thought that deaf people would enjoy these performances. Similar performances have been made by deaf people themselves, unfortunately. J. H. Cripps, Rosenblum, and Small (2016) explained that some deaf performers were prone to the paradigm of music as an audio-centric experience as a result of a poor sense of identity. Such outcome is understandable when considering that some deaf people do not have optimal access to ASL, and are thus restricted by not knowing or being part of deaf culture. The large number of deaf people born to hearing parents who do not learn to sign in their early years (90% - 95%; Lederberg, Schick, & Spencer, 2013; Mitchell & Karchmer, 2005) is a serious matter. It is known that many deaf people learn signed language upon enrolling in a school for the deaf or upon reaching adulthood and meeting other deaf people through the deaf community. Deaf children integrated in local public schools in recent years have their own challenges. The impact of many deaf people not experiencing full enculturation in ASL is part of the reality for the deaf community.

This lack of enculturation includes how deaf performers (listed in the quote above) have used auditory musical instruments and have imitated hearing musicians. (See French (2016) and Jones (2015) for examples of imitation performances). What must be considered is the poor accessibility for deaf people concerning deaf music as compared to signed music. It is true that deaf people enjoy vibrations (as mentioned by Loeffler and Leigh et al.), but this is only one part of the musical experience. Experiencing music through tactility and vibration is simply a means of following the path of audible music. Deaf people will continue to be left out when appreciating the meaning of a musical performance, especially when depending on translation between ASL and English. What deaf people need is exposure to signed music in action. Only signed music can provide a comprehensive and fully accessible musical experience.

In comparison, the musicians discussed in the preceding section, Janis E. Cripps and Pamela Witcher were born to deaf parents and grew up in a signing household in a family with a strong affiliation to the deaf community. This strong background in deaf culture is why these musicians with strong deaf culture backgrounds were selected to study. Moreover, J. H. Cripps et al. (in press) explained that signed music has the quality (in the case of *Eyes* and *An Experiment Clip*) to serve as a natural enculturation and mentorship experience promoting the solidarity of the deaf community. Other deaf musicians born to hearing parents can produce high quality musical pieces when exposed to ASL early in life and taught properly in school about what signed music is, for example.

Finally, the term "deaf music" is narrow in its definition when compared to signed music. Deaf individuals are not the only ones that create signed music performances successfully. There are hearing signers who have created signed music performances as well (e.g. *Earth Move*[3] performed by Sherry Hicks and Michael Velez who were raised in a signing household with deaf parents and are CODAs). The term "signed music" appears to be more socially inclusive as compared to "deaf music." Hearing individuals who have the intention of performing signed music will need to be fluent in ASL and demonstrate respect for deaf culture (i.e., cultural sensitivity; J. H. Cripps et al., in press).

Another term, *visual music,* also needs to be addressed. This term is attractive (as deaf people perform signed music through the visual means), but this term can create confusion. Visual music is popular and in active use among hearing people. Visual music has been reported in the music literature since 1910s. Roger Fry coined this term in 1912 (Zilczer, 2005). During the 1910s to 1920s, visual artists such as Wassily Kandinsky and Frantisek Kupka asserted that their abstract paintings included the nonfigurative structures of musical composition, which paved the way for a new type of art - visual music. Synaesthesia is the concept that visual music artists pursue, incorporating different senses (i.e., smell, touch, taste, sight, and hearing) along with the variety of arts (Strick, 2005). Visual harmony with color aesthetics is one of the most popular properties

---

[3] To view the excerpt of "Earth Move": https://www.youtube.com/watch?v=G9n1L08BWWE

used in visual music. The color composition is what makes the harmony between different colors visually pleasant. For example, DeWitt (1987) used the concept of synaesthesia (i.e., synthesizing hearing and sight into a music piece) when he proposed that "…the piano keyboard is a suitable performance tool for visual harmony; after all, it has become a commonplace as an interface to sophisticated musical synthesizers" (p. 116). Visual music is a genre that used different types of visual arts and Strick (2005) listed them as follows:

- paintings
- photographs
- color organs
- films
- light shows
- installations
- digital media

It is Brougher (2005) who claimed that Walt Disney's 1940 animated-based film, *Fantasia*, is an excellent example of visual music performance. This well-known film was influenced by the work of Oskar Fischinger, a visual music artist during that time. The uniqueness of this film was that it included both lyric and non-lyric songs with artistic visual motion (i.e., animation). Of special interest is the definition that Evans (2005) provided for visual music as follows:

> Visual music can be defined as time-based visual imagery that establishes a temporal architecture in a way similar to absolute music. It is typically non-narrative and non-representational. [It] can be accompanied by sound but can also be silent. (p. 11)

In the silent version of visual music, Evans referred Stan Brakhage's *Mothlight*[4] (created in 1963) as a tonal montage work that incorporated music visually. This montage piece used dead moths and other organic debris from light fixtures. No camera or audible sounds were used and Brakhage included different natural minerals such as twigs, blades of grass, dust, and moth parts into his work. All of these minerals were put onto a sticky tape and printed to celluloid for viewing through the film projector. These plastic materials were cut and placed on the filmstrip to create a fast-paced montage.

In the 'silent version' of visual music, artists do not feel the need to use lyric and non-lyric songs, or any audible sounds. This suggests that some visual music pieces do not require any language or sonic properties. Likewise, deaf individuals can pursue visual music for itself and enjoy a silent rendition.

In addition, hearing, non-signing visual music artists are known for incorporating the lyric and/or non-lyric component(s) into their visual music pieces, using spoken words and/or audible sounds. Deaf individuals can create visual music pieces and incorporate signed words and/or the analogous 'sound system'[5] associated with hand movements. At a minimum, signed music requires

---

[4] To view "Mothlight": https://www.youtube.com/watch?v=Yt3nDgnC7M8

[5] The term sound system commonly refers to personal or professional modes of sonic amplification. These vary from multichannel speaker systems, to body worn devices that privilege sonic tactility (i.e. literally feeling the sound waves through bone induction). In this instance, sound system refers to a mode of amplification that employ visual-

signed language knowledge on the part of the performers. Performers without signed language knowledge will not perform music using their hands and movements sophisticatedly and abstractly like the performances by Janis E. Cripps and Pamela Witcher.

Visual music is not suitable for deafblind people. These people usually rely on their sense of touch to obtain information through their hands (i.e., tactile). They may use tactile signed language (or ASL) to communicate with either sighted or non-sighted peers (e.g., Collins & Petronio, 1998; Quinto-Pozos, 2002). It is likely that the deafblind population will enjoy the musical performances in the signed modality by touching performer's hands in order to follow the hand movements. This contradicts the characteristics and properties of visual music pieces as discussed above. Visual music is best described as inaccessible to deafblind people.

One deaf performer involved with visual music is Rosa Lee Timm, who performed *Tell Your Story* (https://www.youtube.com/watch?v=yfZ8fVf6Ldc). She created this signed music performance that included some of the visual music properties. In this performance, Ms. Timm performed signed lyrics while underwater, with moving air bubbles surrounding her. The bubbles contributed to the visual effect. Along with Janis E. Cripps' non-lyric work, *Eyes* (with its abstract water-like movements), there appears to be a recurring pattern of making references to water. While the perception of sound is dramatically reduced underwater, the performance can still be appreciated through visual means. Another interpretation might be the notion that water is a source of life.

Future Directions

With more awareness and understanding about the concept of music and how it applies to deaf people, it should no longer be necessary to search for appropriate terminology to define this phenomenon. Instead, scholars in various fields (signed language and literature, ethnomusicology, deaf-related studies, and the studies of cognition, aesthetics, and sound) need to move forward by conducting research with existing musical performances to explore the appreciation of the art of signed music. Specifically, using the field of aesthetics as an example, in-depth structural investigation between the distinction of ASL poetry and signed music performances using the performers' use of hands, body and motions should be analyzed. Further investigation of the use of musical elements and motifs in signed music in both contemporary and historical forms is especially valuable for Music Studies.

There are some valuable videos demonstrating signed music available for further study. Cripps et al. (in press) suggested that the availability of these resources will allow a large number of signers to become more educated and conscious of what practices constitute signed music. With greater dissemination, these videos may impact scholars, performers, teachers, and students in their understanding of the characteristics or properties of signed music. In 2015, the Canadian Cultural Society for the Deaf (CCSD) presented an art exhibition on the topic of signed music in its Deaf Culture Center in Toronto, Ontario. Parts of this exhibition were included in a handbook called *Signed Music: Rhythm of the Heart – Deaf Arts Handbook Series Volume II*, which is available online.[6] Also, CCSD produced a 20-minute documentary called *Signed Music: Rhythm of the Heart*.[7]

---

gestural modality that do not rely on an audible source. Further research must be conducted to explain this in greater detail.

[6] http://www.deafculturecentre.ca/Public/Page/Files/642_DeafArtsHandbook_Volume2_FINAL2015-1.pdf

[7] To view "Signed Music: Rhythm of the Heart": https://www.youtube.com/watch?v=FLazgI_phNQ

The first author of this paper produced a documentary in 2016 called *Signed Music: A Symphonious Odyssey*. The documentary was first presented at the Society for American Sign Language conference in November 2015 at Towson University near Baltimore, Maryland. This documentary is available online as well: (https://www.youtube.com/watch?v=2JjFCM8UZHM). A website developed by this author and his colleagues focuses on signed music, including the definitions of each musical element, chronological signed music performances, grants, publications, and presentations (http://wp.towson.edu/signedmusic/). All of these resources available comprise a compilation of artistic works that can be studied as a musical canon. It is the hope of the authors that this paper provides a clear explanation of, signed music and its basis in the theory of language, culture, and music.

References

Akmajian, A., Demers, R. A., Farmer, A. K., & Harnish, R. M. (2010). *Linguistics: An introduction to language and communication* (6th ed.). Cambridge, MA: MIT Press.

Andersson, Y., & Burch, S. (2010). Deaf and disability studies: A conversation with Yerker Andersson. In S. Burch, & A. Kafer (Eds.), *Deaf and disability studies: Interdisciplinary perspectives* (pp. 193-203). Washington, DC: Gallaudet University Press.

Bahan, B. (2006). Face-to-face tradition in the American deaf community: Dynamics of the teller, the tale, and the audience. In H-D. L. Bauman, J. L. Nelson, & H. M. Rose (Eds.), *Signing the body poetic: Essays on American Sign Language literature* (pp. 21-50). Berkeley, CA: University of California Press.

Bauman, H-D. L. (2004). Audism: Exploring the metaphysics of oppression. *Journal of Deaf Studies and Deaf Education, 9*(2), 239-246.

Baynton, D. (1993). 'Savages and deaf-mutes': Evolutionary theory and the campaign against sign language in the nineteenth century. In J. V. Van Cleve (Ed.), *Deaf history unveiled: Interpretations from the new scholarship* (pp. 93-112). Washington, DC: Gallaudet University Press.

Baynton, D. (1996). *Forbidden signs: American culture and the campaign against sign language.* Chicago, IL: University of Chicago Press.

Bender, R. E. (1981). *The conquest of deafness* (3rd ed.). Danville, IL: The Interstate Printers & Publishers, Inc.

Bergman, B., & Wallin, L. (1990). Sign language research and the deaf community. In S. Prillwitz, & T. Vollhaber (Eds.), *Sign language research and application* (pp. 187-216). Hamburg, DE: Signum.

Branson, J., & Miller, D. (1998). Nationalism and the linguistic rights of deaf communities: Linguistic imperialism and the recognition and development of sign languages. *Journal of Sociolinguistics, 2*(1), 3-34.

Brougher, K. (2005). Visual-music culture. In K. Brougher, J. Strick, A. Wiseman, & J. Zilczer (Eds.), *Visual music: Synaesthesia in art and music since 1900* (pp. 88-177). New York, NY: Thames & Hudson.

Brown, H. D. (1994). *Principles of language learning and teaching* (3rd ed.). Englewood Cliffs, NJ: Prentice Hall.

Brown, S., Merker, B., & Wallin, N. L. (2000). An introduction to evolution musicology. In N. L. Wallin, B. Merker, & S. Brown (Eds.), *The origins of music* (pp. 3-24). Cambridge, MA: MIT Press.

Burch, S. (2002). *Signs of resistance: American deaf cultural history, 1990-World War II.* New York, NY: New York Press.

Canadian Cultural Society of the Deaf. (Series author) (2015). *Deaf arts handbook series, vol. 2 – Signed music: Rhythm of the heart.* Toronto, Ontario: Canadian Cultural Society of the Deaf.

Clayton, M., Herbert, T., & Middleton, R. (Eds.) (2003). *The cultural study of music: A critical introduction.* New York, NY: Routledge.

Clayton, M., Herbert, T., & Middleton, R. (Eds.) (2012). *The cultural study of music: A critical introduction, 2nd edition.* New York, NY: Routledge.

Collins, S., & Petronio, K. (1998). What happens in tactile ASL? In C. Lucas (Ed.), *Pinky extension and eye gaze: Language use in deaf communities* (pp. 17-37). Washington, DC: Gallaudet University Press.

Cook, N. (2012). Music as performance. In M. Clayton, T. Herbert, & R. Middleton (Eds.), *The cultural study of music: A critical introduction* (2nd ed., pp. 184-194). New York, NY: Routledge.

Cook, N. (2008). We are all (ethno)musicologists now. In H. Stobart (Ed.), *The new (ethno)musicologies* (pp. 48-70). Lanham, MD: Scarecrow Press.

Cook, N. (2000). *Music: A very short introduction.* Oxford, UK: Oxford University Press.

Cripps, J. H. (2016). *Signed music: A symphonious odyssey* [film]. Towson, MD: A Cripps Production. https://www.youtube.com/watch?v=2JjFCM8UZHM

Cripps, J. H., Rosenblum, E., & Small, A. (2016). Music: Signed. In G. Gertz, & P. Boudreault (Eds.), *The Deaf Studies encyclopedia* (Vol. 2, pp. 702-705). Thousand Oaks, CA: SAGE Publications.

Cripps, J. H., Rosenblum, E., Small, A., & Supalla, S. J. (2017). A case study on signed music:

The emergence of an inter-performance art. *Liminalities: A Journal of Performance Studies, 13*(2).

Cripps, J. H., Small, A., Rosenblum, E., Supalla, S. J., Whyte, A. K., & Cripps, J. S. (in press). Signed music and the deaf community. In A. Cruz (Ed.), *Culture, deafness & music: Disability studies and a path to social justice.* Rotterdam, NL: Sense Publishers.

Cripps, J. H., & Supalla, S. J. (2012) The power of spoken languages in schools and deaf students who sign. *International Journal of Humanities and Social Science, 2*(16), 86-102.

Cripps, J. S., Small, A., Rosenblum, E., & Cripps, J. H. (2015). *Signed music: Rhythm of the heart* [film]. Toronto, ON: Canadian Cultural Society of the Deaf. https://www.youtube.com/watch?v=FLazgI_phNQ

DeWitt, T. (1987). Visual music: Searching for an aesthetic. *Leonardo, 20*(2), 115-122.

Drabkin, W. (2004). Motif. In S. Sadie, & J. Tyrrell (Eds.), *The New Grove dictionary of music and musicians* (2nd ed.). London, UK: Macmillian.

French, M. M. (2016). *A show of hands: The local meanings and multimodal resources of hip hop designed, performed, and posted to YouTube by deaf rappers.* Unpublished Doctoral Dissertation. University of Rochester, Rochester, NY.

Eckert, R. C., & Rowley, A. J. (2013). Audism: A theory and practice of audiocentric privilege. *Humanity & Society, 37*(2), 101-130.

Evans, B. (2005). Foundations of a visual music. *Computer Music Journal, 29*(4), 11-24.

Gannon, J. R. (1981). *Deaf heritage: A narrative history of deaf America.* Silver Spring, MD: National Association of the Deaf.

Geertz, C. (1973). *The interpretation of cultures.* New York, NY: Basic Books.

Hamm, C., Nettl, B., & Byrnside, R. (1975). *Contemporary music and music culture.* Englewood Cliffs, NJ: Prentice-Hall.

Humphries, T. (1977). *Communicating across cultures (deaf/hearing) and language learning.* Unpublished Doctoral Dissertation, Union Graduate School, Cincinnati, OH.

Jones, J. D. (2015). Imagined hearing: Music-making in deaf culture. In B. Howe, S. Jensen-Moulton, N. Lerner, & J. Straus (Eds.), *The Oxford handbook of music and disability studies* (pp. 54-72). Oxford, UK: Oxford University Press.

Kennedy, M., Kennedy, J., & Rutherford-Johnson, T. (2012). *The Oxford dictionary of music* (6th ed.). Oxford, UK: Oxford University Press.

Kramer, L. (2003). Subjectivity rampant! Music, hermeneutics, and history. In M. Clayton, T. Herbert, & R. Middleton (Eds.), *The cultural study of music: A critical introduction* (pp. 124-135). New York, NY: Routledge.

Kramsch, C. (1998). *Language and culture.* Oxford, UK: Oxford University Press.

Lammle, R. (2010). *Roll over Beethoven: 6 modern deaf musicians.* Retrieved from http://mentalfloss.com/article/25750/roll-over-beethoven-6-modern-deaf-musicians

Lane, H. (1984). *When the mind hears: A history of the deaf.* New York, NY: Random House.

Lane, H. (1999). *Mask of benevolence: Disabling the deaf community.* San Diego, CA: DawnSignPress.

Lane, H., Pillard, R. C., & Hedberg, U. (2001). *The people of the eye: Deaf ethnicity and ancestry.* Oxford, UK: Oxford University Press.

Lederberg, A. R., Schick, B., & Spencer, P. E. (2013). Language and literacy development of deaf and hard-of-hearing children: Successes and challenges. *Developmental Psychology, 49*(1), 15-30.

Leigh, I. W., Andrews, J. F., & Harris, R. L. (2016). *Deaf culture: Exploring deaf communities in the United States.* San Diego, CA: Plural Publishing.

Loeffler, S. (2014). Deaf music: Embodying language and rhythm. In H-D. Bauman, & J. J. Murray (Eds.), *Deaf gain: Raising the stakes in human diversity* (pp. 436-456). Minneapolis, MN: University of Minnesota Press.

Maler, A. (2015). Musical expression among deaf and hearing song signers. In B. Howe, S. Jensen-Moulton, N. Lerner, & J. Straus (Eds.), *The Oxford handbook of music and disability studies* (pp. 73-91). Oxford, UK: Oxford University Press.

Meier, R. P. (2002). Why different, why the same? Explaining effects and non-effects of modality upon linguistic structure in sign and speech. In R. P. Meier, K. Cormier, & D. Quinto-Pozos (Eds.), *Modality and structure in signed and spoken languages* (pp. 1-25). Cambridge, UK: University of Cambridge Press.

Middleton, R. (2012). Music studies and the idea of culture. In M. Clayton, T. Herbert, & R. Middleton (Eds.), *The cultural study of music: A critical introduction* (2nd ed., pp. 1-14). New York, NY: Routledge.

Miller, M. B. (1991). *Live at SMI! Mary Beth Miller* [DVD]. Burtonsville, MD: Sign Media Inc.

Mitchell, R. E., & Karchmer, M. A. (2005). Parental hearing status and signing among deaf and hard of hearing students. *Sign Language Studies, 5*(2), 231-244.

Moores, D. F. (1996). *Educating the deaf: Psychology, principles, and practices, 4th edition.* Boston, MA: Houghton Mifflin Company.

Nanda, S., & Warms, R. L. (2002). *Cultural anthropology, 7th edition.* Belmont, CA: Wadsworth/Thomson Learning.

National Theatre of the Deaf. (1973). *My third eye* [film]. Chicago, IL: WTTW Television Station.

Padden, C. A. (1980). The Deaf community and the culture of deaf people. In C. Baker, & R. Battison (Eds.) *Sign language and the deaf community* (pp. 89-103). Silver Spring, MD: National Association of the Deaf.

Padden, C. (2010). Sign language geography. In Mathur, G., & Napoli, D. J. (Eds.), *Deaf around the world* (pp. 19-37). New York, NY: Oxford University Press.

Padden, C., & Humphries, T. (1988). *Deaf in America: Voices from a culture.* Cambridge: Harvard University Press.

Peisner, D. (2013). *Deaf jams: The surprising, conflicted, thriving world of hearing-impaired rappers.* Retrieved from http://www.spin.com/2013/10/deaf-jams-hearing-impaired-rappers/

Petitto, L. A., Langdon, C., Stone, A., Andriola, D., Kartheiser, G., & Cochran, C. (2016). Visual sign phonology: Insights into human reading and language from a natural soundless phonology. *WIREs Cognitive Science.* doi: 10.1002/wcs.1404

Quinto-Pozos, D. (2002). Deixis in the visual/gestural and tactile/gestural modalities. In R. P. Meier, K. Cormier, & D. Quinto-Pozos (Eds.), *Modality and structure in signed and spoken languages* (pp. 442-467). Cambridge, UK: Cambridge University Press.

Rutherford, S. (1988). The culture of American deaf people. *Sign Language Studies, 59,* 129-147.

Sandler, W., & Lillo-Martin, D. (2006). *Sign language and linguistic universals.* Cambridge, UK: Cambridge University Press.

Saville-Troike, M. (2003). *The ethnography of communication: An introduction* (3rd ed.). Oxford, UK; Blackwell.

Schmidt-Jones, C. (2007). *Understanding basic music theory.* Houston, TX: Connexions & Rice University.

Schuchman, J. S. (1988). *Hollywood speaks: Deafness and the film entertainment industry.* Urbana and Chicago, IL: University of Illinois Press.

Stokoe, W. C. (1960). *Sign language structure: An outline of the visual communication systems of the American deaf.* Studies in Linguistics: Occasional Paper 8. Buffalo, NY: University of Buffalo.

Strick, J. (2005). Visual music. In K. Brougher, J. Strick, A. Wiseman, & J. Zilczer (Eds.), *Visual music: Synaesthesia in art and music since 1900* (pp. 14-22). New York, NY: Thames & Hudson.

Supalla, C., & Supalla, D. (1991). *Short stories in American Sign Language* [VHS]. Colton, CA: ASL Vista Project.

Supalla, S. J., & Cripps, J. H. (2008). Linguistic accessibility and deaf children. In B. Spolsky, & F. Hult (Eds.), *The handbook of educational linguistics* (pp. 174-191). Oxford, UK: Blackwell.

Supalla, T. (1994). *Charles Krauel: A profile of a deaf filmmaker* [VHS]. San Diego, CA: DawnPictures.

Sutton-Spence, R., & Woll, B. (1999). *The linguistics of British Sign Language: An introduction.* Cambridge, UK: Cambridge University Press.

Thaut, M. H. (2005). *Rhythm, music, and the brain: Scientific foundations and clinical applications.* New York, NY: Routledge.

Traugott, E. C., & Pratt, M. L. (1980). *Linguistics for students of literature.* San Diego, CA: Harcourt, Brace, & Jovanovich.

Valli, C., Lucas, C, Mulrooney, K., & Villanueva, M. (2011). *Linguistics of American Sign Language: An introduction* (5th ed.). Washington, DC: Gallaudet University Press.

Van Cleve, J. V. (Ed.) (1993). *Deaf history unveiled: Interpretations from the new scholarship.* Washington, DC: Gallaudet University Press.

Van Cleve, J. V., & Crouch, B. A. (1989). *A place of their own: Creating the deaf community in America.* Washington, DC: Gallaudet University Press.

Zilczer, J. (2005). Music for the eyes: Abstract painting and light art. In K. Brougher, J. Strick, A. Wiseman, & J. Zilczer (Eds.), *Visual music: Synaesthesia in art and music since 1900* (pp. 24-86). New York, NY: Thames & Hudson.

Zeshan, U. (2000). *Sign language in Indopakistan: A description of a signed language.* Philadelphia, PA: John Benjamins.

Is Silence Music to the Eye?
A Review of *Signed Music: A Symphonious Odyssey*

Lisalee D. Egbert
American Society for Deaf Children

On November 15, 2015, Towson University had the honor of hosting *Signed Music, A Symphonious Odyssey*. As one of the conference participants, I had the privilege of viewing this evening performance and would like to share my experience and thoughts with insights. The video production of this evening performance can be viewed at https://www.youtube.com/watch?v=2JjFCM8UZHM. The notion of signed music has been a concept that has led to controversy among many researchers and educators in Deaf Studies. The idea of including music as a discipline within Deaf Studies has been fiercely debated in recent years. It has been suggested that music has no place in the Deaf community and that music is a wholly "hearing" notion which is not applicable to Deaf culture, thus there is no purpose in researching its ideology. On the other side of the argument, there are scholars whose work demonstrates and documents a long history of how signed music has always been embedded in Deaf culture.

Given the accessibility and visual ease afforded by the Internet, the output of visual media is overwhelming and raises many questions: Is music a hearing-only concept? Is music simply an auditory aspect of life? Can music be a visual notion? Can music be considered as Deaf art or literature?

When William Stokoe's work suggested that American Sign Language (ASL) was indeed a language (Stokoe, 1960; Stokoe, Casterline, & Croneberg, 1965), researchers both Deaf and hearing, as well as lay persons, were quick to condemn his work (Maher, 1996). Accepting ASL as a legitimate language took time in both the research and the Deaf communities. Acknowledgment was slow possibly because, as humans, we are reluctant to accept change. We tend to drive the same route to work, we tend to eat primarily the same foods, and we frequent the same venues. But is it deeper than that? Are we disinclined to accept new concepts because we are creatures of habit and thereby resist change? Or, are we perhaps myopic in our paradigms because *we do not want to accept what, at some level, we consider to be strange or different?*

Much of the academic community, as well as the Deaf community, has now accepted Stokoe's work through which he demonstrates that the linguistic features of ASL meet the criteria of a language. Language is rooted in culture and culture is woven in language (Brown, 1994; Kramsch, 1998). Deaf Studies as an academic discipline emerged from Stokoe's revolutionary linguistic breakthrough. Over time Deaf Studies as a university major was established, followed by the granting of university degrees (Bauman, 2008). A natural progression for the field would be to explore further layers of the cultural and linguistic aspects of its discipline.

Now that Deaf Studies has been acknowledged as a legitimate academic field, research pursuits have begun to proliferate. Deaf Studies scholars have documented the advent of not only Deaf art and literature, but subcategories within art and literature. For example: the performing arts of theater, poetry, and storytelling are acknowledged subcategories within "Deaf Literature" (Peters, 2000). These are joined by visual arts such as painting, sculpture, and more. These explorations in Deaf art, poetry, and literature are not new phenomena, but until there was formal and proper apperception by the academy, researchers did not investigate the potential of these categories. None of this was "new" to the Deaf community, but rather, these arts were woven into the fabric of ASL and Deaf culture, merely waiting to be explored.

To date, scholars in the field have described a foundation of Deaf Studies by noting aspects of storytelling, poetry, linguistics, and cultural studies. Researchers have since catapulted into a variety of further investigations within Deaf Studies. Researchers examining the layers of language and culture can observe the vibrant complexities and discern differences that once were not identified. Bahan's (2006) publication on the topic of storytelling serves as an excellent example. It has been noted that Deaf Studies has always examined storytelling. Scholars now more closely analyze storytelling and note that there are, in fact, different types of storytelling in ASL. Recently, it was determined that the umbrella label of storytelling is just the face of an art that needs further study. As a result of Bahan's (2006) work, ASL storytelling is recognized as having many genres, including narratives, cinematographic stories, folktales and more, not merely the traditional conceptualization of storytelling. Bahan's publication updates William Stokoe's research from the 1950s and 60s. Had Bahan simply accepted the traditional "storytelling" model, the research community would not see the gestalt and complexity of the art of storytelling. Storytelling is one example of how the study of Deaf cultural arts is expanding.

The evening performance of *Signed Music: A Symphonious Odyssey* was a professional encounter that provided the audience with a reminder that our field is in its infancy. There is much to absorb and investigate as researchers in Deaf Studies. Just as our sister disciplines of history, psychology, and anthropology, while significantly more established research areas than Deaf Studies, are still making inroads in their domains, so is Deaf Studies. This performance *also* provided an opportunity to encounter Deaf Studies through various perspectives and to examine a framework through which experts explore our own language and culture.

Signed music, by its very name, raises numerous questions. What is it, exactly? Who is employing signed music? Is signed music a production by and for the Deaf community, or is the hearing community capitalizing on a trend? Clarifying on what signed music is, a group of scholars defined it as:

> "…wholly autonomous from the auditory experience. While it is pleasing to the eyes, just as conventional music pleases the ears, it has parameters that are completely different from musical forms hearing audiences are used to, such as audible pitch. Specifically, a high-quality music performance (without words) includes handshape variations along with unique movements like circles, motioning up-and-down, back-and-forth, or to-and-fro representing possible notes. Some performances also include lyrics or "words" in ASL." (J. H. Cripps, Rosenblum, Small, & Supalla, 2017 p. 4)

In what ways is Deaf culture embedded, woven, and interlaced in signed music? Is signed music some type of audism mask? Audism is frequently defined as the oppressing view of ability to hear over inability to hear as well as the view of the superiority of spoken language over signed language (Bauman, 1994; J. H. Cripps & Supalla, 2012; Eckert & Rowley, 2008). Is our lens colored by dysconscious audists? (See Gertz, 2008 for the concept of this type of audism). Are Deaf Studies scholars paying attention to the crab (theory) network of Deaf community members who cannot acknowledge sound research in the field, much less that the research is valid? Does the word "music" itself insert some sort of logophobia into the Deaf community? If the construct did not utilize the word "music," might it be more readily accepted?

Signed Music: A Symphonious Odyssey provided an opportunity for cultural and musical growth across communities with an interest in Deaf Studies. The conference, hosted by the Society for American Sign Language at Towson University in Maryland, provided numerous opportunities to explore, examine, and tease out disparities in aspects of signed music, ASL poetry, and storytelling. The day-long event was well-attended by national and international researchers, undergraduate and graduate students, Deaf community members, Children of Deaf Adults, parents of children with Deaf children, Deaf artists, and more. The day began with presentations on research in Deaf Studies and ASL. Presenters offered insights into sign language, as used in the United States and Canada. Videos featuring both Deaf and hearing artists had been prepared prior to the conference to be shared with the participants. Discussion was presented on storytelling, poetry and … signed music.

When interacting with both Deaf and hearing professionals in the field, the most common and substantial misconception is that "signed music" is when a person tries to apply ASL or signed words to mainstream hip-hop, country or any type of instrumental music with lyrics. In terms of signed music, this is not at all the case because of the cultural and linguistic differences between English and ASL (see J. H. Cripps, Small, Rosenblum, Supalla, Whyte, & J. S. Cripps, in press for further details on the concept of signed music related to cultural norms).

Spectators of *Signed Music: A Symphonious Odyssey* were afforded the privilege of having signed music explained in presentation form, and performed both on-screen and in live performance. The forum showcased accomplished artists who graced the audience with their signed music performances and poetry. Historic videos were shown. Live theater was enacted. Audiences experienced a gamut of emotions from amusement to sadness. At one poignant segment, the assembly experienced clear confusion followed by absolute understanding.

Toward the end of the performance, Dr. Jody Cripps dressed to conduct a symphony with white gloves and a tuxedo. The camera focused on his hands. The symphony began, and yet, his hands did not move. We waited. Still no movement. At first, there were little grins in the crowd suspecting a technology malfunction. Still no movement. The audience members began to look at each other. Still no movement. After a considerable amount of time, his hands awoke and signed, "Would that be considered music? That's what is up for discussion." Is "nothing" music to some? Is silence music to the eye? To my Deaf eye, a silent eye would be death.

Researchers have begun to perform their due diligence by exploring the research and publications on the topic of signed music. Authors like Jody Cripps, Anita Small, Ely Rosenblum, Samuel Supalla, Aimee Whyte, and Joanne Cripps have produced analyses outlining the merits of signed music. The author(s) provide definitions, examples, patterns, and rules, in addition to current and historical accounts of signed music. These writers have conducted substantial research (J. H. Cripps, Rosenblum, & Small, 2016; J. H. Cripps et al., 2017; J. H. Cripps et al., in press).

William Stokoe's work had value that was initially ignored. Scholars did not attend workshops or read journal articles to guide them in the groundbreaking notion that ASL was a language. If William Stokoe, Ben Bahan, and others' work had gone unnoticed or uninvestigated by other researchers, where would the ASL and Deaf community be in the state of our own research and discipline now? As a research community in Deaf Studies, it is scholars' obligation to explore and understand signed music. From a research standpoint, academics must keep exploring *all* components of the abundance of avenues in our Deaf community and signed language.

From a practical application, signed music can play a valuable role for families with Deaf children, as well as in Deaf Education. The American Society for Deaf Children (ASDC) is the oldest parent-to-parent organization in the United States whose purpose is to support, encourage and provide information to families who are raising Deaf children. ASDC recognizes the critical role of families who set the tone for their children in terms of education, language, culture and more. ASDC supports Deaf Education programs that embrace ASL and English equality and are open to ideas that will scaffold a Deaf child's creativity while concurrently balancing ASL and Deaf culture. The American Society for Deaf Children encourages families and educators to capitalize on a child's strengths. If a Deaf child was interested in exploring music visually, it would behoove the child to watch signed music. Videos such as Rosa Lee Timm's *River Song* (2008) and *Tell Your Story* (2014), as well as Janis Cripps' *Eyes* (2003) can be used to enhance appreciation for visual arts, introduce and showcase Deaf culture, and enhance the self-esteem of Deaf children. Families with Deaf children can simply enjoy "the arts" together by talking about the signed music pieces and find inspiration together. Time for families to bond together in ASL and learn about Deaf people and their community is essential. Promoting family togetherness in ways that provide language accessibility build self-esteem in a child, provide a foundation of security for the child, and more, much more. Having a family that not only celebrates a Deaf child, but also includes cultural and linguistic features for the child, is monumental.

Acknowledgement

Special acknowledgment to Georgia Nemeth in preparing this article.

References

Bahan, B. (2006). Face-to-face tradition in the American Deaf community: Dynamics of the teller, tale, and audience. In H-D. L. Bauman, J. L. Nelson, & H. Rose (Eds.), *Signing the body poetic: Essays in American Sign Language literature* (pp. 21–50). Berkeley, CA: University of California Press.

Bauman, H-D. L. (2004). Audism: Exploring the metaphysics of oppression. *Journal of Deaf Studies and Deaf Education, 9*(2), 239-246.

Bauman, H-D. L. (Ed.). (2008a). *Open your eyes: Deaf Studies talking*. Minneapolis, MN: University of Minnesota Press.

Brown, H. D. (1994). *Principles of language learning and teaching, 3rd edition*. Englewood Cliffs, NJ: Prentice Hall.

Cripps, J. E. (2003). *Eyes*. Tucson, AZ: A Janis Furlong Production. https://www.youtube.com/watch?v=YnwJsFHFebg

Cripps, J. H. (2016). *Signed music: A symphonious odyssey* [film]. Towson, MD: A Cripps Production. Retrieved from https://www.youtube.com/watch?v=2JjFCM8UZHM.

Cripps, J. H., & Supalla, S. J. (2012). The power of spoken language in schools and deaf students who sign. *International Journal of Humanities and Social Science, 2*(16), 86-102.

Cripps, J. H., Rosenblum, E., & Small, A. (2016). Music: Signed. In G. Gertz & P. Boudreault (Eds.), *The Deaf Studies encyclopedia, Vol. 2* (pp. 702-705). Thousand Oaks, CA: SAGE Publications.

Cripps, J. H., Rosenblum, E., Small, A., & Supalla, S. (2017). A case study on signed music: The emergence of an inter-performance art. *Liminalities: A Journal of Performance Studies, 13*(2): 1-24. (http://liminalities.net/13-2/signedmusic.html)

Cripps, J. H., Small, A., Rosenblum, E., Supalla, S. J., Whyte, A. K., & Cripps, J. S. (in press). Signed music and the deaf community. In A. Cruz (Ed.), *Culture, deafness & music: Disability studies and a path to social justice.* Rotterdam, NL: Sense Publishers.

Eckert, R. C., & Rowley, A. J. (2013). Audism: A theory and practice of audiocentric privilege. *Humanity & Society, 37*(2), 101-130.

Gertz, G. (2008). Dysconscious audism: A theoretical position. In H. D.L Bauman (Ed.), *Open your eyes: Deaf Studies talking* (pp. 219-234). Minneapolis, MN: University of Minnesota Press.

Kramsch, C. (1998). *Language and culture.* Oxford, UK: Oxford University Press.

Maher, J. (1996). *Seeing language in sign: The work of William C. Stokoe.* Washington, DC: Gallaudet University press.

Peters, C. (2000). *Deaf American literature: From the carnival to the canon.* Washington, DC: Gallaudet University Press.

Stokoe, W. C. (1960). *Sign language structure: An outline of the visual communication systems of the American Deaf, Studies in linguistics: Occasional papers (No. 8).* Buffalo, NY: Dept. of Anthropology and Linguistics, University of Buffalo.

Stokoe, W., Casterline, D., & Croneberg, C. (1965). *A dictionary of American Sign Language on linguistics principles.* Silver Spring, MD: Linstok Press.

Timm, R. L. (2008). *The Rosa Lee show.* [DVD]. Rosa Lee & Damon Timm.

Timm, R. L. (2014). *Tell your story.* https://www.youtube.com/watch?v=yfZ8fVf6Ldc

www.ingramcontent.com/pod-product-compliance
Lightning Source LLC
Chambersburg PA
CBHW081849170426
43199CB00018B/2862